MW00928968

UNTOUCHABLE

*-reaching the most despised
with God's love*

Tabitha B. C. Abel

Names have been changed to protect the privacy of individuals.

New International Version (NIV) Bible translation is used for scriptures

unless otherwise indicated.

Copyright © 2017 Tabitha B. C. Abel
tabithaabel@yahoo.com
All rights reserved.

ISBN: 978-1536 833102

Cover picture: dream_designz

Publisher: The Association for Sexual Abuse Prevention,
Printer: CreateSpace, Charleston, SC

DEDICATION

UNTOUCHABLE – reaching the most despised with God's love is dedicated to those who want to understand pedophilia and so reduce child sexual abuse by helping pedophiles *before* they act on their attraction. We hear the cries of children who have been sexually abused and are working towards decreasing child sexual abuse by learning about Untouchables –pedophiles. *UNTOUCHABLE* is dedicated to making the world a safer place one child at a time, one pedophile at a time and one sinner at a time through Jesus Christ's healing touch. Jesus offers to all healing, forgiveness and the power to "go and sin no more".

"Silence is the friend of abuse." Anonymous

ACKNOWLEDGMENTS

UNTOUCHABLE – reaching the most despised with God's love would have never been written had Gary (Gibson), my husband, not encouraged and inspired me by his commitment to preventing child sexual abuse through our on-line ministry for non-offending pedophiles through the Association for Sexual Abuse Prevention (ASAPinternational.org). Thank-you Gary for putting me straight when I was confused and for allowing me to write long sentences, even though you like short ones!

My thanks also to Nancey and Jean who ploughed through what I wrote even when they weren't convinced that what I said was right. Your questions and suggestions made me think again before it was too late and your editorial skills made *Untouchable* a better read. Thank-you. My thanks also to Helen who made me re-focus my writing.

Thank-you to Jesus Christ for using me to reach others for His kingdom. My prayer is that all who read *UNTOUCHABLE* will choose to accept the healing touch of Jesus Christ no matter what their sin is, and "go and sin no more".

Tabitha B. C. Abel
In His Service

CONTENTS

CHAPTER 1

WORSHIPING WITH THE SAINTS

No one doubted their sincerity. They were almost twenty individuals who were committed to living lives in harmony with God's will –in as many different ways. No two were alike.

Ken, the discussion leader asked, "Friends, what *is* the 'Great Controversy' and when did it start?"

"It's about the war between good and evil," one said.

"It's about Satan and Jesus," said another as heads nodded in agreement.

"Good," Ken said. "The Great Controversy started before the beginning of time —when Satan decided that he wanted to be more than a created angel, even though he was the Archangel, the Highest Angel in heaven. That wasn't good enough for him. He wanted to be worshipped and adored like God. His jealousy was the start of evil. He wanted to rise above his station and follow his own way."

Ken paused, "Let's turn to Isaiah 14:12-14 and see it in black and white. We'll find that sin originated in Satan's heart, or rather in his head."

Pages rustled briefly as the congregation turned to Isaiah.

"Satan had an 'I' problem. A big 'I' problem," Ken said. "This led to a rebellion in heaven. Let's pick it up at verse 13. 'I will ascend to heaven; I will raise my throne above the stars of God...I will ascend above the tops of the clouds; I will make myself like the Most High.'

"Satan was all about himself and when the seed of pride took root in him. It grew like cancer and resulted in a full blown rebellion in heaven."

Ken was right. Even though it was impossible to fully explain how sin came to be, it was enough to know, as the Bible says, "That you (Satan) were blameless in your ways from the day you were created till wickedness was found in you (Ezekiel 28:15)." Satan was a created being but he chose to sin against God.

Ken continued. "At the end of the Bible, in Revelation 12, John, one of Jesus' disciples tells the story of the dragon (Satan) attacking the woman (the church). The woman was about to give birth to a son (Jesus Christ). It depicted war. The dragon made every effort to destroy the Child when He was born. You remember that at the time of Jesus' birth many babies were killed by King Herod in Bethlehem when, under Satan's influence, Herod ordered all boys under two years to be killed. He planned to kill anyone who might threaten his throne. The killing had been prophesied by Jeremiah (Jeremiah 31:15) and it was the Wise Men who actually reminded Herod of the prophecies about the Messiah's birth."

Ken paused, "Does anyone remember what then happened?"

Bethany's hand shot up, "God warned Joseph in a dream that King Herod wanted to kill Jesus and an angel told Joseph to take Mary and Baby Jesus and escape to Egypt (Matthew 2:13). Then the angel came to Joseph again and said that it was safe for them to return to Israel because Herod was dead. According to historians, those verses cover two or three years."

"Yes Bethany, and it also seems that 'the angel of the Lord' was Gabriel, the angel who superseded Satan, AKA Lucifer, in heaven. What Gabriel did –tell Mary she was to give birth to baby Jesus, announce Jesus' birth to the shepherds and give Joseph instructions to flee to Egypt for safety, would have been Satan's job had he not rebelled and been thrown out of heaven (Matthew 10:18). What a thought!"

Ken continued, "Revelation 12:9 pulls everything together by calling the dragon, the Devil, that serpent, Satan. Satan was in heaven before the beginning of planet Earth's history and was at war with Michael (another name for Jesus) and lost the battle (Revelation 12:7). Then he and his rebellious followers, the angels he had deceived, were cast out of heaven to Earth."

Satan was *the* deceiver. He deceived many angels. He deceived Eve into eating the forbidden fruit in the Garden of Eden, and Adam right after her. The story about the first sin on Earth is on page two in my Bible, but who could say it didn't happen 200 years after the Earth was created? The Bible tells us that before sin happened both Adam and Eve talked face-to-face with God the Father.

They could have been talking for a few centuries. Who knows? They certainly understood that they could eat from all the trees in the Garden except from one. God set a boundary that they were not to cross. They understood that. They had more than enough fruit to satisfy their physical needs. The fruit rule was to test their love for Him. He said, "You are free to eat from any tree in the garden; but you must not eat from the tree of the knowledge of good and evil (Genesis 2:16,17)." Only that one tree was out of bounds and it stood next to the tree of life, in the middle of the garden.

Adam and Eve were smart. Their minds hadn't been blighted by centuries of sin. They were noble, perfect, intelligent personal friends of God, their Creator. They understood what He said and yet God gave them the opportunity to choose for themselves. They had freedom of choice. God wanted mankind to obey Him out of love, not because they had to. They weren't mindless automatons controlled by their Creator. It is likely that God, like a loving Father watching over His children, told them many times to keep away from the tree of knowledge of good and evil for their own good, explaining that when they ate from it, they would "surely die".

"I think of a hot stove when I consider this story," Ken the discussion leader said. "Most of us have told our children not to touch something hot because we love them, and don't want them to get hurt. And what do they do? When our backs are turned, they touch it. Now they know what being burned is all about, but it is too late. They knew we loved them, but still chose to disobey us."

"Eve was no different. First she loitered near the forbidden tree and then she started to converse with that incredible, talking snake. It enticed her into a web of lies. 'Did God really say that you must not eat from any tree in the garden?' (Genesis 3:1). He put doubt into Eve's mind. Parleying with the enemy is always a bad idea. Captivated, she told the snake exactly what God had told her adding that she should not even touch it, 'or you will die' (Genesis 3:3). Conciliatory as women often are, she defended God not realizing that she was standing on the Devil's ground. Why was she even near the forbidden tree in the first place?"

"Satan, the Father of Lies, was ready and told her a whopper. She would *not* die when she ate the fruit (Genesis 3:4) he said, and then followed it by a second lie. If she ate it, she would 'be like God'. Probably Satan handed her a piece of fruit. He was living evidence that touching the fruit did not kill him. She took a bite –and didn't die instantaneously, but something *did* start to die within her when she disobeyed God. Eve didn't understand death as we do now, but the blight of that first sin was enough to feel something new, something bad."

"It appears that Eve had wandered away from Adam and was on her own when she got into conversation with the Devil, but we know she then gave the fruit to Adam, and he took a bite too. Perhaps she went to find him, or maybe he suddenly realized she wasn't with him and he went looking for her. Perhaps Adam loved Eve so much that he ate the forbidden fruit with his eyes wide open. Whatever the case, Adam took the fruit and ate too. Then they both knew they had disobeyed God and began to feel loss for the very first time."

"Sin successfully took root in the Garden of Eden as Eve, and then Adam, chose to believe Satan's sophistries over God's instructions. The rest of the Bible records a loving God repeatedly warning His people of the consequences of choosing to disobey, rather than obey Him.

Sin progressed rapidly from that first sin, to the

murder of Abel by his brother Cain (Genesis 4: 1-15). Wickedness continued to flourish until the time of the flood (Genesis 6-8) when all but Noah and his family were saved in the deluge. On down through the ages people turned their backs on God and when God's Son came to this planet to rescue it, He was not recognized. The Old Testament prophecies were overlooked and eventually He was crucified as a common criminal in fulfillment of other prophecies."

"Satan focused his attention on Jesus' life on earth. It was his golden opportunity to obtain the planet for himself and make man his eternal captive. He didn't mind how it happened. He just had to be successful. He would use King Herod, the scribes or Pharisees and the religious leaders to accomplish his goal. Anyone. He tempted Jesus in person in the wilderness (Matthew 4, Luke 4), but failed to get Jesus to worship him, or to use His God-given powers to benefit Himself. If Satan could have made Jesus sin even once, Satan would have become the master of this world. This was serious war and Satan planned to win it. He was in conflict with Jesus from Jesus' first breath as a baby, to His last breath when He cried out on the cross, 'It is finished (John 19:30)'. Those triumphant words sealed

Satan's fate and gave us hope and the opportunity of everlasting life. The sinless Son of God had paved a way for us to get back the perfection that was lost in the Garden of Eden."

The congregation nodded in agreement. They were born-again Christians. They knew they were in line for heaven with Jesus because they had accepted His offer of eternal life. In time they would reap their reward. Praise the Lord. They were almost ready for translation! *Really?*

Ken pulled them back to his first question. "So …what is this controversy? What is it all about?"

Patsy held up her hand, "It is an incredible story that shows us that God really does love us."

"You're right Patsy," Ken said. "and not just our planet –the whole universe. Friends, there is so much we do not know but we must believe that God loves us, wretched sinners that we are." Ken paused. "We really *do* have a sin problem here on Earth, so what should we do when we come face-to-face with it?"

As saints almost ready for translation to the heavenly realms it was unlikely that they would come face to face with sin, they foolishly believed. Sin wasn't attractive to them, usually. They chose their friends carefully. They didn't wear provocative clothing and never frequented bars or strip clubs. They didn't do drugs, steal or murder. They lived healthfully, not indulging in too much ice-cream or fast-food, and many had adhered to their own exercise programs, most of the time. They read their Bibles daily –often. Their marriages were solid, not supremely happy perhaps, but solid and satisfying. Going on-line to find a relationship on the side was totally out of the question and divorce would never happen again. They would never go down that path again. There had been no sordid tales of sin about any of the saints sitting in the pews recently. Granted, one of them was missing because of a rather suspect situation, but the congregation was holding fast to the truth.

"What sins are you willing to tolerate in others –or yourself?" Ken asked. "We know that God is a God of love. The apostle John tells us this many times in his three little letters, 1st 2nd and 3rd John, near the end of the Bible, and twice in 1 John 4 he says 'God is love' (1 John 4:8, 16). If God loves us that much, surely He will over-look little sins?"

The congregation was quiet. Talking about sin was uncomfortable. Bethany, a trim, exercise fiend finally spoke up, "The Bible says that gluttony is a sin –but I would welcome obese people worshiping with me."

Coral, a sweet, heavy-set lady raised her hand, "I think we all have hidden sins that we don't advertise when we walk through the door," she said. "You can't see thoughts. Who is to say that being obese is worse than thinking bad thoughts towards other people? Like wishing someone would get cancer or suddenly be in a horrible motor accident and come face to face with their mortality –and the unlikelihood of getting to heaven? Perhaps God allows bad things to happen so that they *will* come to their senses and find Him. I think that anyone thinking evil thoughts, or lying, or stealing from their office, or gambling –or whatever, needs to come and sit next to me in church. I want 'em here."

Coral had a point, but perhaps Ken could steer the discussion away from these touchy subjects. But he did not.

"Would those sins put sinners in the same league as murderers, perpetrators of domestic violence or child sexual abusers, sex addicts, druggies or porn addicts, homosexuals and transgenders and the like?" Ken asked. "Surely these sinners would be headed for that lake of fire written of in Revelation 21:8?" Ken paused. "And what would *you* do if a transgender person, or a cross-dresser came to worship with us in our church?"

Mike was ready, "That happened a few months ago in a friend's church," he said. "A few complained to the pastor that people wearing women's clothing were going into the women's restroom, but they weren't women. Parents wanted to know what to tell their children. It was very confusing," he said. "In the end, the pastor decided that transgenders and cross-dressers shouldn't come to church at all. So they left."

Quickly Bethany interjected, "Well, my question is about gays coming to church. Do we let them come and sit with us or not?"

Ken had discussed just such a scenario with his wife earlier that week. One church in the community had refused to let an openly gay lesbian sing in the Christmas program and another church leader told them that they were not welcome until they stopped being in an open, gay relationship. Stop your sinning, and then you can join us, they were told.

"So what *should* we do if they came here?" asked Ken. "The Bible tells us in Leviticus 18:22 'Do not lie with a man as one lies with a woman, that is detestable.' That tells us that homosexual practices are sinful, whether in a loving relationship or not. But shouldn't we invite them in and treat them with respect and kindness?"

Charlie, a new believer spoke up quickly, "Of course they should come Ken. I know God created Adam and Eve, and not Adam and Steve, but which one of us doesn't sin in some way every day? Who's to say someone with one type of sin should worship with us while someone with another sin should not? You just said we *all* have a sin problem, and no one is beyond the reach of God."

Murmurs of approval surfaced. Charlie was on a roll, "And besides, we are told not to judge. We are to leave it up to the Holy Spirit or God, or someone. I don't know where –but the Bible says it somewhere."

"You're right. We are not to judge. It's in Luke 6:37," Ken said, "and if we keep our eyes on Jesus and accept what He has done for us, then we will become like Him. The Holy Spirit convicts people of their sins. We should let Him do His job."

"Then they can *sit* beside us," interjected Patsy. "But we shouldn't have people who aren't living according to biblical standards teach our Bible class. Right?"

"Right, Patsy. Nor would we invite someone who has been imprisoned for embezzlement to be the church treasurer. We need to love the sinner, like Jesus did, without loving the sin itself."

Out of the corner of his eye Ken saw George raise his hand. He knew what was coming. George chatted on-line with the worst of the worst sinners, pedophiles. He knew George was all about preventing child sexual abuse, but he also knew that George was probably going to invite pedophiles to come and worship with them.

"Based on what you said Ken," George started, "we should welcome *pedophiles* to our church. Not *child-molesters*," he added, "they are not one and the same you know."

Ken had been told that before. However, George was getting on his hobby horse and this time Ken wasn't going to be caught napping.

"George, we know about your on-line ministry, and many of us don't agree with you. We know you want to prevent child sexual abuse and we know your thoughts about this, but pedophiles are pedophiles, and we do not want them here in our church."

Ken paused, "This has been a long discussion and

I see the time has run out."

Phew! If George got on his favorite topic, the prevention of child sexual abuse and pedophilia there would be no stopping him for a very long time. George should give up trying to convince everyone. There were limits as to who should be accepted into their congregation, and pedophiles weren't on that list.

CHAPTER 2

UNTOUCHABLE?

C hristian communities the world over are like this little church. They are faced with difficult questions regarding sexuality and lifestyle, and are usually ill-prepared to deal with them. Liberal/progressive Christians tend to welcome everyone into fellowship while conservative/legalistic Christians have an eye for rules and interpret scripture according to their theological forefathers, or more robustly.

JUDGING ONE ANOTHER

Many Christians want to possess the character qualities called the fruit of the Spirit found in Galatians 5:22,23. These characteristics are "love, joy, peace, patience, kindness, goodness, faithfulness, gentleness and self-control." Against this list Christians may unscientifically measure their own personality traits in an effort to determine their degree of holiness, and their readiness for translation to the heavenly kingdom! Some may ask the Holy Spirit to give them a divine make-over while others will be satisfied with their spiritual standing.

In Psalm 139:23 David invited God to read his heart (thoughts) but John, in the New Testament writes that it is the Son, not the Father, who has been entrusted with the job of judging. Jesus said: "Moreover, the Father judges no one, but has entrusted all judgment

> **No person, not even the most respected Christians, can rightly determine the thoughts and motives of others.**

to the Son … And He (God) has given Him (Jesus) authority to judge because He is the Son of Man (John 5:22, 27)." Clearly, no person, not even the most respected Christian, can rightly determine the thoughts and motives of others.

A clear case of misjudgment was recorded in John 8. John was the only gospel writer to record the story of the scribes and Pharisees bringing a woman caught in adultery to Jesus. They hoped to catch Jesus out, that

Itinerant Preacher they so detested. Would Jesus obey Moses' law and stone the adulterous woman, or ignore the law?

"Now Teacher, what are *you* going do, *eh*?"

The contemptuous woman had been caught in the act of adultery, obviously with someone who they chose not to bring to Jesus. Women were so low on their totem pole of respect that it didn't matter if she died for *her* sin. However, bringing the man with whom she was sinning to justice might jeopardize their upward mobility, and so they ignored him.

Many church goers will have seen this story enacted and relish the outcome. They anticipate the vivid downfall of the conniving, self-confident, hypocritical leaders who looked on the cowering, loose woman with contempt.

Jesus ignored them –apparently. The Bible says, "Jesus bent down and started to write on the ground with His finger (John 8:6)."

So they needled Him as He continued writing in the dust. In time, "He straightened up and said to them, 'If any one of you is without sin, let him be the first to throw a stone at her (John 8:7).'"

Jesus had outwitted them! He knew the law very well and what would be her punishment according to their laws, but He wasn't into condemning repentant sinners. He could read her heart.

John wrote that the scribes and Pharisees departed one at a time, from the oldest to the youngest, leaving the woman alone with Jesus. With the audience now gone Jesus said, "Neither do I condemn you; go now and leave your life of sin (John 8:11)." Some authors suggest that Jesus wrote a list of her accusers' sins in the dust and as they read them they felt convicted, and shamefacedly departed.

What sins would Jesus be writing in the dust had modern Christians been her accusers?

Some propose that the woman caught in adultery was Mary Magdalene, Simon's niece, the Simon in whose home Mary poured expensive perfume on Jesus' feet shortly before He was crucified (Matthew 26:6-13; Mark 14:3-9). They suggest that Simon, a prominent man in society, had molested his niece and set her on the pathway to sexual promiscuity. But whatever the case, would Christians today invite her to sit next to them in church or are they, like the scribes and Pharisees of Jesus' time, so busy looking for specks in everyone else's eyes that they miss the huge beam in their own eyes?

Jesus did not condone her actions. He did not say, "Go home, my dear. I forgive you. It's okay."

Without being judgmental, He told her to slip away and leave her sinful life. He, a person without sin, did not publicly berate her. As the perfect Son of God, it was His right to judge her but Jesus was not about the business of shaming and humiliating others. He told her that adultery was wrong, but His actions were uplifting, not condemnatory.

A MODERN PHARISEE AND TAX COLLECTOR

Jesus told a story about a so-called righteous Pharisee, and a pathetic, sinful tax collector praying at a distance from the temple. It is found in Luke 18:10–14. Today someone who is in good and proper standing in the church might boldly pray, "Oh God, I thank-you for making me who I am. I worship You each week and fulfill my duty as church elder with sincerity. I teach Bible classes and support the church with my finances. I am content with my Mercedes, my state of the art I-phone® and an Apple® watch. I lack nothing. My home alarm system keeps my family safe. I do not beat my wife for she does as I tell her. I have attended AA meetings faithfully for more than 12 years even though I might have a tipple with the governor on New Year's Eve. City council meetings keep me busy but I am not morbidly obese and have never been to a strip club, although I might glance occasionally at soft-porn on the internet when my life is challenging. I don't smoke and take only prescribed medications. I never mean to cut people off on the freeway and I am good to my staff. Thank-you Lord for making me me. I honor you."

And the tax collector, or a less-than-acceptable person might almost inaudibly say, "Forgive me for my sins Lord, and show me Your way. I need Your help. I can't make it on my own."

Would we be surprised that the less-than-acceptable person received God's blessing and the revered church-goer was not recognized by the Lord? To the supposedly righteous Christian, Jesus might say, "I never knew you. Away from me you evildoer(s)! (Matthew 7:23)"

UNCLEAN, UNCLEAN

Some of the people most loathed in Jesus' day were lepers. They were kept outside the cities and had to fend for themselves. They had to call "unclean, unclean" and ring their jingling bells to keep people away. They were social outcasts. They were untouchables, like the lowest castes in India. Unclean, sinful and untouchable. With our advanced medical knowledge, we know that most lepers in Jesus' day did not actually have Hansen disease (leprosy) as we know it, but likely other skin diseases. When "leprosy" was first mentioned in Leviticus, isolation precautions were instituted by God to avoid contagion and this persisted in Jesus' day with even greater distain because leprosy was regarded as a punishment from God. Jesus, however, regarded lepers as destitute human beings with physical, emotional, social and spiritual needs. He disregarded the health laws of the day and *touched* these so-called sinful, ugly people—and healed them, to the horror of both the crowd and His disciples.

> **Jesus regarded lepers as destitute human beings with physical, emotional, social and spiritual needs.**

Dr. Luke records Jesus healing a group of ten lepers (Luke 17: 12-19), of which one was a Samaritan. Jesus granted their request for healing and ordered them to go and be examined by the priests, as was customary. As they went on their way they were healed. What is so remarkable is that only one of the ten turned around and went back to Jesus to thank Him and glorify God. And he was the Samaritan, an enemy of the Jews, a person looked upon by the Jews as dirt on the bottom of their sandals. But the Samaritan thought that thanking Jesus was more urgent than being given a clean bill of health by the priests. That could wait. Expressing his thanks couldn't.

JESUS' COUNTER-CULTURE VALUES

Jesus went against the culture of the day by healing lepers. He touched lepers too, although this is not directly stated in some healings. However, in Luke 5:12-16 Jesus' touch healed a leper and Mark writes that Jesus healed many who *touched Him*, "as many as had plagues (Mark 3:10 KJV)." No doubt these were untouchables also, and yet Jesus did not run from their touch. Rabbinical literature testifies that in Jesus' day healing a person of leprosy was considered as difficult as raising a person from the dead.

Jesus practiced counter-culture godliness. He respected women, including a Samaritan woman at the well

> **Jesus practiced counter-culture godliness.**

at Sychar (John 4: 5-30). He healed a woman who had endured menstrual problems for 12-years, and who was therefore regarded as unclean (Luke 8:43-48) and one of His final thoughts on the cross was for His mother's safety after His death. He commissioned John to care for His mother's needs (John 19:26,27). Jesus blessed children who were brought to Him who other religious leaders (and His disciples) thought were unimportant, and one of Jesus' most remarkable miracles was bringing Jairus' 12-year-old daughter back to life (Mark 5:22-24, 35-43; Luke 8:41-42, 49-56). Children were important to Him.

Jesus validated women, children, lepers and other lowly people who were considered unimportant by the leaders of His day. These actions gave His followers cause to carefully consider the worth of a human soul and yet, despite Jesus' example, they were slow to recognize the worth God sees in everyone, whether of apparently high or low esteem.

TODAY'S "LEPERS"

The auditorium was mesmerized by a dramatic presentation: A "leper" hobbled down the aisle to the platform. Banished from society, he no longer provided for his family and had not felt the touch of a human hand for seven years. Swathed in dirty bandages, tinkling his bell and crying "unclean, unclean" as he mounted the platform with difficulty, he turned to face the audience. The congregation gasped. Weeping facial sores were partly covered by dirty bandages.

But as the story unraveled the congregation realized it was an enactment of a true story with a happy ending. The actor portrayed the leper Jesus healed and the bandages, bell and disgrace fell away. The leper rejoiced. He was healed and could re-enter society in full health once again –and the congregation relaxed.

Then the pastor turned to the congregation and asked, "Who are today's lepers? Who have we banished from society? Who are the most unwanted, hopeless and despised people in today's society?"

Christians believe that Jesus would have given His life for just one, single lost soul because He saw no one as being hopeless, worthless or unwanted. However, most people turn away today's "lepers," –those with a pedophilic orientation.

> Minor attracted people are undoubtedly the most detested members of today's society.

"We do not want you. You are not part of our family," they say.

How can Christians morally justify this treatment of people cursed with a sexual orientation nobody wants? Minor attracted people are undoubtedly the most detested members of society. They are stigmatized and automatically labelled as child molesters, and denied the remotest hope of being one of God's children.

Christians do not, and should not condone child molestation at any level. Jesus was very clear when He said that it would be better for someone who offends "one of these little ones" to have a large millstone hung about his neck and "be drowned in the depth of the sea" (Matthew 18:6). Abuse is unacceptable, however, by equating men and women who are sexually attracted to children as outcasts from society (and church), so called Christians are behaving like the temple leaders of Jesus' day who assumed leprosy was a judgment from God for sinful actions, while revering long prayers as an indication of a sanctified, God-fearing heart. Christians must not make similar assumptions for lack of knowledge.

CHAPTER 3

OUT OF THE TOY-BOX AND INTO THE FIRE

Sexual sin is no longer hidden. Turn on the news, stroll through your town in the evening or eaves drop on college kids or friends chatting at a bar. It leaves no doubt in the mind that sexual sin has taken root in our communities. Sexual sins and behaviors such as rape, prostitution, adultery, burlesque and adult entertainment, strip clubs, sex slavery and LGBT (lesbian, gay, bisexual, transgender) issues are rampant, and even visible at some check-out stands at the grocery store. Other sexual sins are more accessible and no less insidious, such as digital pornography, sexting and other on-line sexual activities.

But Untouchables –pedophiles or minor attracted people, are still made synonymous with child molesters, which is simply *not* an accurate conclusion. Currently pedophiles are the most despised members of our community. They disgust all but perceptive people who are beginning to ask what pedophilia *really* is, and question whether every child molester is a pedophile.

In a world where truth is relative, lust is pampered, right is unpopular and bad means good, there is growing confusion. Christians should make it their responsibility to understand the nuances of pedophilia and not just follow public opinion. A knowledge of their state's sex offender (S/O) laws will also help Christians make informed decisions in these matters before arbitrarily judging pedophiles as Untouchables who should be locked up.

Ignorance does not remove the responsibility from faith communities to judge impartially, and with understanding, but many faith communities have never considered this matter because it does not impact them. Unfortunately, that truth is "relative" because many are already impacted by it, yet do not know it –yet.

PEDOPHILES ARE PEOPLE

For most people the word "pedophile" conjures up the image of the most recent child molester's mug-shot seen on the local TV station, because the words "pedophile" and "child molester" are unfortunately used interchangeably. A growing group of unsavory child molesters who prey on innocent children are viewed as the lowest, most corrupt, disgusting collection of humanity possible –but should they be equated with pedophiles?

A brief lesson in etymology, the study of language, tells us that "ped" refers to "child", originally from ancient Greek where it meant "boy, child". We use it in words like "pediatrics", the medical treatment of children, or "pedontics," a branch of children's dentistry. In the 17th century "pederasty" described "sodomy of a man with a boy" but it is no longer used. "Philo" is an ancient Greek root word meaning "loving, fond of, tending to" as well as "friend" and "to love". And so the word "paedophile" (English), or "pedophile" (American English) was coined in the early 1950s to refer to a person who had a sexual attraction to children. Pedophiles who have not acted on their attraction (and never wish to) are justifiably fearful to seek help because most people assume them to be child molesters. Additionally, their own children may be taken away from them by Child Protective Services (CPS), if they have them, and they may suffer unjust treatment by the law if they reveal their inner fears despite having done nothing unlawful.

The American Psychological Association, the American Psychiatric Association and other medical professions state that everyone is entitled to compassionate, non-judgmental healthcare and yet this does not happen for

> **Pedophiles are stigmatized, and portrayed as devious, manipulative, non-humans.**

those with a pedophilic orientation. Pedophiles are stigmatized, and portrayed as devious, manipulative, non-humans. Finding non-judgmental therapists can be challenging but by stereotyping pedophiles as shameful, worthless, sociopathic monsters with no conscience, makes pedophiles feel hopeless, and very fearful of seeking help in case they blow their cover or are even suspected of being a minor-attracted person (MAP). Pedophiles still have almost no voice despite a wealth of new research showing that these assumptions are incorrect. However these emerging findings give a glimmer of hope.

There is a *huge difference between having a pedophilic*

sexual attraction, and acting on that attraction, but society is still very skeptical of any pedophile who hints that they are living a good, decent life. They are assumed to be lying.

HEALTHY BODY, MIND AND SPIRIT

Christians are taught that their "body is a temple of the Holy Spirit" (1 Corinthians 6:19) and they are encouraged to keep their bodies pure, free of sinful desires and physically healthy for the Lord to dwell within them. Jesus paid for each person's salvation with His life and, as His temple they should "therefore honor God with their body (1 Corinthians 6:20)." A healthy mind, body and spirit is an attainable goal.

The US and other resource rich nations may be referred to as "temptation nations" because rich foods, chocolate and fast food is mouthwateringly attractive and available. Citizens know that these foods contain harmful fats, cholesterol and calories that put health at risk for cardiovascular diseases, breast, prostate, colon and many other cancers, and obesity, to name a few lifestyle health problems. But for many they are irresistible, that is until an acute coronary incident occurs. Many, scared by near-death, develop a backbone and resist the mouth-watering German chocolate cake placed in the middle of the dessert table! With stents placed in their coronary arteries (or worse), some may finally quit smoking *and* drive past their favorite fast-food joint leaving the diet soda, triple cheese burger and fries out of their diet forever. They successfully step towards better health and decrease their risk of many diseases.

Alcoholics and drug addicts can also get clean and live free of their addiction. But society continues to believe that "once a pedophile, always a child molester" is true. There is something radically wrong with this reasoning.

> God created man with the power of choice. Everyone can make smart choices.

Getting the victory over a fast-food addiction (at some level) is an illustration of people's ability to make purposeful, good choices with respect to strong habits, and even addictions. Choosing whether to act on a sexual urge or not, comes under the same umbrella—choice. God created man with the power of choice. Everyone can make smart choices, especially with Divine help.

SOCIETAL CHANGE

Adam and Eve were created sexual beings with a sexual drive to love one another. God's purpose was that they should have children and "fill the earth" within that loving relationship between a man and a woman. In the 1970s society tampered with the purpose of marriage by giving women the choice to have children, or not. It was called The Pill. Later, people were able to sign a contract, not a covenant as a Biblical marriage is, with someone of the same gender and be childless, or choose alternative, scientific methods to bring children into the partnership and become a family like hetero-sexual couples. Society's norms have now so changed that the moral compass is no longer pointing north. This is part of Satan's plan to destroy the family unit as it was originally given by God to our fore parents, Eve and Adam, and to infiltrate as many families as possible with his deceptions.

> Society's norms have so changed that the moral compass is no longer pointing north. This is part of Satan's plan to destroy the family unit as it was originally given by God to our fore parents.

Everyone is born into an imperfect world with physiological, emotional, psychological, spiritual and sexual imperfections inherited from past generations. Unfortunately, it is easier to edge towards the dark side than towards God's perfection. With comparative ease people imperceptibly drift away from God unless they keep their eyes fixed on Jesus. The cosmic war between good and evil, the Great Controversy, is in accelerated action and yet God still gives people the freedom to choose right over wrong and good over evil just as He did in Eden.

PEDOPHILIA

Many scientists believe that MAPs (pedophiles) have an *inborn* attraction to prepubescent children. It is not an acquired attraction. In several recent anonymous studies, one in four college-age men acknowledged some sexual interest in children, and at least 10% of adult men continued to experience some level of sexual attraction to children (Goode, 2010).

Nearly everyone begins their sexual journey with an attraction to children but most people's sexual attraction changes as they age. People with pedophilia continue to have a sexual preference for children who are usually in a specific age range, and of a specific gender. Cloud (2003), in an article titled "Pedophilia", states, "According to Dr. Fred Berlin, a Johns Hopkins University professor who founded the National Institute for the Study, Prevention and Treatment of Sexual Trauma in Baltimore, Md., pedophilia is a distinct sexual orientation marked by persistent, sometimes exclusive, attraction to prepubescent children."

Very few pedophiles are exclusive and sexually attracted only to children. Many pedophiles develop also mature sexual relationships with adults, in which the adult sexual relationship is their primary sexual orientation, and the sexual attraction to children is secondary. Most MAPs/pedophiles agree that they did not choose their sexual orientation and that they do not want it, but they cannot cut it out of their genetic make-up just as eye color is genetically inherited and unchangeable.

How might the emerging pedophile, who is usually in his teens, feel about an unwanted sexual attraction to children? Confusion about one's sexual orientation is widespread in teens, especially if they feel they are not "normal" sexually. Simply put, psychologists say that a sexual orientation is an enduring expression of sexual desire, over time, whether heterosexual (towards the opposite gender), homosexual (towards the same gender) or a paraphilia, which refers to a group of unnatural sexual attractions and includes pedophilia.

Having a homosexual orientation is no longer as terrifying as it was a decade ago, but if sexual feelings are aroused towards young children while the normal, hormonally-charged feelings are *not* being felt towards peers of a different gender, or the same gender, then this is cause for concern in any adolescent. Extremely confused, a chilling awareness of pedophilia starts to grow and they begin to believe they are monsters with perverted sexual urges which they try to hide. Utterly ashamed and with nowhere to turn, they assume there is no way out and they will become a full-blown child molester, because that is what public opinion says. Without support and information this can be more than they can bear and can quickly lead down a dark, dangerous path to depression and suicide. How should they deal with this problem? How would we?

Occasionally people dream the same scenario time and again. They find themselves repeatedly unable to run away from a monster, reliving a traumatic situation in the battle field, unable to fly to safety as they fall off a cliff or some other frightening situation. Just when their end is in sight, they wake up in a sweat and find themselves lying in a tangled mess of sheets in their own bed. The relief is overwhelming as they realize it was a nightmare and their pulse returns to normal.

For the pedophile, their dream is an inescapable, living nightmare from which they will not awake.

Over time the teen's confusion turns into a sexual awareness that confirms that he, and it is most often a male, is not sexually normal. The terrifying reality that he is a pedophile sets in. It may be akin to falling off a cliff and not being able to fly, because the only pedophiles he knows are the

> For the pedophile, their dream is an inescapable, living nightmare from which they will not awake.

child molesters (often incorrectly labelled "pedophiles"), who have been caught doing dirty things with prepubescent children and who have lost their marriages, homes, jobs, children and/or reputation, and are going to jail for a very long time, as described in news reports. The teen believes that they will join these social outcasts, the scum of society and believe that they are unlovable, defective and profoundly disgusting. That is what society, the police force and many social workers believe.

THE QUANDRY

So who can they turn to? To a counsellor who is a mandatory reporter? To their pastor, who is also a mandatory reporter and may not know the nuances of their state's laws? The pastor may assume he should report a teen's confusion about his sexuality to the authorities while, in reality, he has nothing to report as nothing has happened. The fine print contained in each state's laws about child sexual abuse are complex, and often difficult to interpret and when so much is as stake, such as this teen's life-long reputation and the possible formidable impact on his family, errors should not be made because of ignorance. Few teens speak of their fears to their parents either. Most mothers would not know where to turn for help and be scared-spitless that she has a child-molester in her house where there might be younger siblings and step-siblings. She would be petrified that if she said something to anyone in authority, her child would be taken off to juvie, or worse.

A married man may have been having these nightmares over months, or years, but does not know where to turn. He may want to come out to his wife but he is too fearful that it will destroy their marriage. He fears also that his family will be dragged through the court of public opinion and that he will be locked up for years, never able to return to a normal life. Also, how would his siblings and parents accept him if he told them the truth?

Strongly suspecting pedophilia, the pedophile's desire to roll over in bed and go back to sleep is enticing because the alternative, waking up and facing the painful reality, is too scary. This self-awareness may be referred to as "coming in" to the realization and is an important step in their journey. Others, ignoring the obvious, may decide that a better way to deal with their sex drive would be to slit their

> **The pedophile's desire to roll over in bed and go back to sleep is enticing because the alternative, waking up and facing the painful reality, is too scary.**

wrists, or lie down on the railroad tracks before they act on their attraction or confess to someone out of desperation. Revealing their secret could be worse although their self-hatred may be suffocating them. Eventually, just as gay people "come out of the closet" and reveal their homosexual orientation, so pedophiles may decide to announce their sexual attraction to children, which is often referred to as to "coming out of the toy-box".

THE REALITY

A sad realization for emerging pedophiles to learn is that society, the courts, CPS, law enforcement, parents, friends of the family, colleagues at work or school or church, all believe that there is no hope for today's Untouchables and that they should be locked up with the key thrown far, far away to some irretrievable place. The Christian community can become knowledgeable and a safe place for non-offending pedophiles who seek treatment and need support before they act on their attraction. No one wishes to experience *their* nightmare.

Mark's situation is a sad illustration of what can happen. Failing to find help for his pedophilia, Mark molested his niece at a family gathering –but no one knew about it. He was overcome with shame, regret and disgust at his own behavior and was so fearful that he would molest another child that he committed suicide. Death was better to Mark than the future he saw ahead of him.

> To reduce the incidence of child sexual abuse, professional help must be accessible to pedophiles and support given to them to stop them from acting on pedophilic sexual urges before they start.

It is no wonder that severe depression and attempted, and successful suicides, result from the hopelessness MAPs feel. Society must understand that to reduce the incidence of child sexual abuse, professional help must be accessible to pedophiles and support given to them to stop them from acting on pedophilic sexual urges before they start. Hatred never brings healing. Hatred makes it more likely that pedophiles will molest a child because of fear, loneliness, a poor self-image, isolation and desperation and laws that have the practical effect of limiting access to professional help for pedophiles, drives would-be molesters underground, and tends to make them more likely to commit crimes against children.

The Christian community, the public at large and MAPs need to know that there is a huge difference between sexual attraction and action, and child abuse is not inevitable. It is preventable.

The following words were posted on-line anonymously and entitled *"My Deepest Secret."*

> *"My entire life I have lived with a secret. I have actively hidden it from everyone that I know for as long as I can remember and sharing it with anyone has always been unthinkable. To me, sharing this feels like putting a loaded gun to my head, giving you the trigger and hoping you don't pull. Now the die is cast.*

> *"I did not choose to be like this. I feel trapped, isolated, alone, and most of all I feel a great deal of shame. We are all at the mercy of our neurochemistry; none of us can change how our brains are wired. I have lost the biochemical lottery; I have a brain that is different than most and I would give anything to change it.*

> *"I have always wished things would change, that I might 'grow out of this'; however, this has not been my experience. To my frustration, over the years, my neurochemistry has remained mostly unchanged. My only current option: to do my best to live a good and virtuous life despite my*

*unfortunate cognitive reality. I have not, and will not, allow
my secret to define who I am.*

*"I am enthusiastic, compassionate and curious. My brain
is probably 99.99% the same as everyone else, but in that
0.01% my secret lies. Most nights I lie awake agonizing
over the question: Why am I so different? I still don't
know the answer.*

*"As you read this, I feel the cool, hard barrel of that gun
press hard against my warm forehead. I feel your finger
slowly wrapping around the ready trigger. Tighter now. My
life in your hands – no turning back, no way out – my
deepest secret brought to light. I brace myself as I stand on
the edge and take a slow, deep breath, cool air filling my
lungs, my heart beating uncontrollably. Will you pull the
trigger? I roll the dice.*

*"Who am I? I am a compassionate but flawed person with
good intentions who never wants to allow my inner demons
to takeover. I struggle to live by the better angels of my
nature.*

"My secret. What am I? I am a pedophile."

This case study is not an isolated incident but one
of thousands of stories about the fear and unwelcome
reality people experience if they are sexually attracted to
children.

It is time for the Christian community to unpack
the truth about pedophilia, and enable pedophiles to get

help to not act on their attraction. Christians will then be part of the action to reduce the incidence of child sexual abuse in our communities.

CHAPTER 4

IDENTIFYING PEDOPHILES AND CHILD MOLESTERS

Everyone is God's unique creation and can be an independent thinker. Christians are encouraged to uphold truth and not rush to judgement – but sometimes fail. They are like the people in the little church who were quick to judge while being ignorant of the facts. Christians may feel awkward judging others knowing that God can see the log in their eyes even as they examine the speck in their quarry's eyes (Luke 6:41,42), but when faced with questions about sexuality (or pedophilia), ignorance cannot be an excuse for condemnation. Certainly Christ's followers should not run afoul of the biblical principles of judging inequitably because they lack the tools to become informed, unbiased decision makers. Too often, discussions on healthy sexuality are swept under the carpet, which is then tacked down. God asks people to form opinions with deliberation and not to rush to judgement without consideration of the true facts.

CLASSIFICATION OF UNTOUCHABLES

A simple, organization of levels of pedophilia will assist in understanding pedophilia especially with respect to reaching Untouchables with God's love. These levels are not scientifically tested.

Level 1: Untouchables with a pedophilic orientation who have not acted on their sexual attraction to children and who care deeply about children are in this category. They never wish to act on their attraction and are the main focus of this book.

Level 2: Minor attracted persons who have acted on their sexual attraction, feel huge guilt and disgust at their behavior and have no desire to step over the line again are clustered in Level 2. They have caused no real trauma to a child but they are filled with self-hating and are distressed. These may or may not have been adjudicated and they may have not been prosecuted or convicted. Their desire is to return to Level 1 functioning but fear they may molest and fall into Level 3.

Level 3: These are the most feared group of people who may not have a pedophilic orientation but who are likely to be narcissistic and evil, seeking their own sexual pleasure without regard to the damage they impose on children and on any one with whom they associate whether spouse, family, church friends or whatever. These are psychopathic criminals who are antisocial and manipulative, using others to obtain their desired outcome. They account for approximately 1:20 of sexual offenders in jail and are in a league different from the two other groups. They warrant the name "sexual molester" and worse, but as Christians we must try to recognize them, difficult as it may be, as children of God, for whom Jesus was willing to give His life. A difficult call, no doubt. These, when identified, have severe psychological, psychopathic and/or emotional disturbances and it is unlikely that readers will be able to restore these people to full psychological health. These people need to be removed from society, receive S/O treatment and never be allowed to interact with children alone. They prey on the innocence of Christians, women who are desperate for support because of the struggles they are going through –especially if they have children, on vulnerable children and anyone who will serve their purpose. This group is referenced in UNTOUCHABLE, but their plight is likely to exceed the capabilities of the lay public.

Unfortunately pedophiles are not categorized according to Levels in real life and more often all are automatically thought of as Level 3 pedophiles. This is a problem. Moving down from one group to another happens, but a greater understanding of where a specific, non-offending pedophile stands, is important. UNTOUCHABLE addresses the difficulties pedophiles face and gives some insight into the lives of MAPs in each group.

SEX OFFDENDER REGISTRY & STATE LAWS

Regular teens often sexually interact with each other but in the US they may not know that what they are doing may put them on the S/O registry for life. Regulations vary considerably between states and jurisdictions, (and by the judges passing sentence), so it is impossible to accurately predict an outcome. Some jurisdictions differentiate between teen and adult offenses with respect to placement on the S/O registry.

Interacting sexually with a child who is more than 5-years younger than the abuser is considered abuse whether the abuser is 19 years old (adult age), 14 years old or 11 years old. In these cases a power differential exists.

A 19 year old sexually interacting with a 16 year-old girl-friend commits statutory rape in some jurisdictions, although it is unlikely the adult will be prosecuted. Technically, this is a matter for mandatory reporting as a "child" is involved and cannot legally give consent. It is unlikely that every such couple would be reported –unless the child's family did not like the "abuser". It would be very unusual for a female aged 19 to be reported when the male is 16 years old, although two 13 year-olds have been prosecuted for sexually interacting with each other even though it was an amicable relationship.

Should a 15 year-old who sexually interacts with a nine-year-old cousin at family gatherings, or in their home on a number of occasions, end up on the S/O registry even if the child enjoyed the sexual attention and did not feel abused by it or think that is was wrong? Should the abuser be on the registry for 10 years or life? Today there is discussion that a life-sentence on the registry from the age of 15 or 11 years of age is unrealistic, but the law requires mandatory reporters to report what happens and then leave it to the "system" to deal with the outcome. However, society at large, and Christ's followers whose goal it is to protect children, should recognize that the system needs to be reviewed so that "sin" they committed at 12-years of age, does not have to impact them every day for the rest of their life. In 2016 judges are calling for a review of sex-offender laws (Singal, 2016).

It would be helpful if there was consistency in state laws for sex crimes so that what is legal on one side of a state border is not illegal, with far reaching consequences, a few hundred feet away in an adjacent state. This may be the result of the differing age of consent by up to two years (16 to 18 years) or for more complex reasons. How does one deal fairly with these arbitrary differences? Is this scientific, or reasonable, and what should society do about it? Can we clearly determine which person accused of sexually abusing a "child" is a pedophile or a narcissistic child molester? Should all be reported? Who should or should not be placed on the S/O registry? These are hard questions and the responses can be confusing.

Ultimately each case must be taken individually and

take into consideration the fact that the DSM-5 recognizes that an older adolescent in an on-going romantic relationship with a 12 to 13 year-old person may be acting illegally, but is not being abusive (American Psychiatric Association, 2013, p. 697).

Abducting a child from a park is a rare occurrence perhaps because the "stranger danger" media blitz of the last 30 years has worked well, or because it was a misguided declaration from the start. The "stranger danger" campaign is no longer promoted as a strategy that is effective in significantly reducing child abuse in the US. Approximately 115 cases of child abduction and molestation from parks occur each year (Akerman, Harris, Levenson, & Zgoba, 2011), which can be compared with nearly 100,000 *substantiated* child molestation cases annually. But child molesters and pedophiles can be easily overlooked as society believes them to be strangers moving in different circles from them.

Unfortunately, the greatest danger of child molestation comes from within the home and *anywhere* regular people congregate.

GETTING RID OF PEDOPHILIA

People with a sexual attraction towards children

do not want this attraction but they cannot wash it off, or pray it away. Well-meaning Christians may suggest that homosexuals should "pray the gay away", but there is little evidence to support that it works. However, those who choose a gay life-style for convenience could have a different outcome. However, instructing a pedophile to pray pedophilia away is not a sure-fix either. Prayer though can help control the actions of a true homosexual or pedophilic person, while not changing what may be their genetic make-up.

The Bible says that we can be "partakers of the divine nature (2 Peter 1:4 NKJV)", but God does not promise to change a person's sexual orientation in this life. People who sincerely seek to

> **Prayer can help control the actions of a gay or lesbian person, or a pedophilic person, while not changing their genetic make-up.**

avoid the negative actions associated with their sexual orientation by putting their trust in the Lord, will no longer be alone in their battle against acting out on their unsanctified sexual desires. Specific counseling strategies, with prayer and Bible reading, can help a person minimize, and manage his or her same gender, or pedophilic attraction.

ACCESSING HELP

It is well for the faith communities to consider whether the laws under which they live, actually help or hinder a person with pedophilia to access professional counseling or community support. In general MAPs recognize that laws in most jurisdictions work against them accessing help

> Regulations are more likely to push MAPs underground and into depression and fear, and so increase their risk of acting-out their worst nightmare.

through both professional and non-professional avenues. In fact the regulations are more likely to push MAPs underground and into depression and fear, and so increase their risk of acting-out their worst nightmare. Should churches follow suit and treat these people as Untouchables based on federal, state and local jurisdiction laws? Like us, MAPs are sinners born into a sinful world and it is time for the Christian community to take a new look at this problem and its solutions. The church can be that touch of hope.

CLASSIFYING PEDOPHILIA

There are two classifications of pedophilia according to the DSM-5: pedophilic disorder and pedophilic sexual orientation. DSM-5 is the bible for the diagnosis of psychological disorders. Psychologists, physicians, mental health counsellors and health care providers usually have a copy, even though many will disagree with certain particulars in it.

Respected expert on livestock, professor, scientist, consultant, author and public speaker Temple Grandin (Grandin & Panek, 2013) does not mince her words when writing about the DSM-5 with respect to autistic spectrum disorders. The newest classification for Aspies puts them in a "social communication disorder" which is "rubbish" (p.110) according to Grandin who further says that, "To me, DSM-5 sounds like diagnosis by committee. It's a bunch of doctors sitting around a conference table arguing about insurance codes (p. 113)." If that happens with autism and Asperger syndrome diagnoses, it might be the same for pedophilia. No wonder professionals don't agree.

Less than 5% of the male population have a pedophilic disorder. To be classified as such, these people must be at least 16 years old and at least 5 years older than the child about whom they have had recurrent, intense sexual behaviors, fantasies, or urges about over a period of at least six months. These emotions have resulted in them experiencing marked interpersonal distress –or they have acted on those feelings.

Those with the less concerning pedophilic sexual <u>orientation</u> experience the same feelings, but are not distressed by these experiences and have not acted on them. It is unlikely that any of this type of MAP will molest a child, but society tells them otherwise.

GENDER ISSUES

Girls are more likely to be sexually abused than boys, while boys are less apt to report any sexual interaction with an adult because frequently they do not consider it abuse. It is fairly common knowledge that perpetrators who molest boys admit to molesting an average of 120 male victims, whereas those who molest girls acknowledge an average of seven victims. These figures come from self-disclosure. We can only conjecture why these differences occur.

> Most convicted S/Os are not molested as children and most victims will not become S/Os.

Women sexually abuse both boys and girls but much less frequently than do men, and it is less likely to be reported to the authorities. Many will be care-givers working in day-care centers, nurseries or hospitals where their prey may be very young and unable to report and the back-ground check made when applying for the position was clear as there was no record of convictions. Likely they had moved strategically to avoid detection. Female convicted S/Os account for between 5-20% of sexual offenders, more often considered about 10%. It is to be noted though that 37-43% of all prison inmates in the US are S/Os (Jensen, 2016). Jensen also stated that most convicted S/Os were not molested as children but acted out sexually when they were kids, and enjoyed it.Most victims will not become S/Os

About 10% of the general population self-identify as being gay, however, among the male, minor attracted, non-offending population, around 50% are attracted to boys. This does not mean that those who are attracted to boys are necessarily more likely to act on their attraction than if their attraction had been to girls, but boys may be more accessible, less likely to report and therefore the behavior is more likely to persist. We should note though that this on-line data also reports that these minor-attracted, non-offending men do not primarily identify themselves as gay.

PATHWAYS TO PEDOPHILIA

There is more than one pathway to pedophilia. A

prenatal trait, as recognized by many researchers, may be stimulated by environmental elements such as incidental situations in childhood, or adverse childhood experiences, including sexual abuse. Broomhall (2016) proposes that three reasons may account for pedophilia: 1) Pedophiles have been abused in the first place; 2) Pedophiles have stalled sexual development because they have developed neither social nor sexual relationships with their peers, choosing rather to withdraw from society in general and participate in relationships and activities on-line; or 3) they were born pedophiles. There is growing support in research and psychological communities for this last option, although the first two options may well be contributing factors.

Some medical text books display photographs of infants with genetic disorders or syndromes. People with specific diseases have a certain look about them. This may be part of their journey toward a correct diagnosis and an effective treatment plan being developed for them. But can one identify a pedophile in a similar way?

Pedophiles look like anyone else. They are men – or women. Tall, stout, skinny, muscular, handsome or awkward. They are professors, store clerks, teachers, counsellors, physicians, computer-geeks, college students, parents, adolescents, farmers, between jobs, laborers et cetera. They surf, go back-packing, play video-games, eat pizza and go to clubs. They attend church, city hall meetings and are on committees. Some choose to work with kids, and others deliberately avoid being around them. They can be friendly and normal –except that inside they all hide the fear that someone will eventually find out that they have a pedophilic orientation.

It would be remiss to omit a reference to the associations found by some researchers between developing dysfunctional sexual behaviors, including pedophilia, with faulty bonding in infancy and early childhood, and deviant fantasies and behaviors in later childhood. Attachment theories follow the premise that humans have a natural propensity to form emotional bonds which begin in infancy.

Quinn (2015) supports research by Finkelhor and Marshall that found sexually deviant behavior coming from a combination of psychological, developmental and biological factors, including deviant sexual arousal, few or poor attachments and loneliness (p. 145).

"Wouldn't it be great," Quinn asks, "if it were

possible to reduce the amount of molestation in our society by identifying individuals who have potential to commit such acts and get them help before they do those things (p. 143)?" Wouldn't it?

ATTRACTION

Minor attracted people generally acknowledge that their sexual attraction becomes manifest during adolescence and that there are many variations of sexual attraction. Just as most teliophiles (adults who are attracted to adults) know whether they are attracted to males, females, or both, so most pedophiles can easily identify the age and gender of their attractions. Pedophiles may identify themselves as having a specific age of attraction (AOA) and gender attraction. Some may be exclusive (sexually attracted only to prepubescent children), while other MAPs have a primary sexual attraction to children and yet may be in a satisfying sexual relationship with an adult of the same or different gender. Still others may have a secondary sexual attraction to children.

Gender plays a major role in their sexual attraction and while some pedophiles may be attracted only to children of one gender, others may have a secondary attraction to children of the other gender in a completely different age range. However, a disproportionate number of men (nearly half) are sexually attracted to boys even though they may be also sexually attracted to adult women. So do they *have* a homosexual, heterosexual or bi-sexual sexual attraction or *is* that what they *are*? Finally –are they gay? The jury is out on that one.

MONSTERS OR NOT?

Many pedophiles believe they are monsters even before others broadcast this lie about them, hence overwhelming guilt and fear lies hidden inside them. Recognizing that they have such a reviled imperfection produces extreme self-loathing and plummeting self-esteem. But all pedophiles do not turn into child molesters (monsters) –even though some do, and those who molest children, are not necessarily pedophiles. What is important to remember is that a pedophile has a sexual interest (at some level) to children of a certain AOA, whether or not they act on it, whereas child molesters molest children regardless of what motivated them.

In real life, most children are attracted to pedophiles because pedophiles naturally work well with kids and are fun to have around. Hence many VPs (virtuous pedophiles –people who have a pedophilic orientation but have not acted on their attraction) like to teach school, volunteer in boys' and girls' clubs, church youth groups etc. After volunteering they may realize that the pleasure they get from working with kids has an undergirding sexual attraction. This realization may evolve over time and become an unwelcome consciousness. However, a number of MAPs maintain that being around children, with other adults present, actually reduces the risk of them sexually interacting with a child. For others, it is the opposite.

CHILD MOLESTERS, LEVEL 3

Let's take another look at child molesters. They are often narcissistic, immoral people who molest children for situational reasons such as not having a willing sexual partner, lack of conscience and having a power-hungry, evil nature. It is these molesters that give the pedophilic population a worse name than they deserve. Or the child molester may be a pedophile who has gone awry, moving from Level 1 to Level 2, because they have not been able to access help and have not learned to deal with their sexual attraction safely. Abel & Harlow (2001) believe that 95% of *convicted* child molesters are pedophiles, however others' research indicates that less than 50% are pedophiles.

Clearly there are discrepancies.

Research on *convicted* child S/Os shows that half of them are family members living with the child, and may be a parent, step-parent or sibling of some form, and a further 30% are relatives who are not living with the child. Another 10% of child sexual abusers are known to the family, leaving only 10% of child sexual abusers as being strangers (Abel & Harlow, 2001). Tabachnick & Klein (2011) proffer that 80% of child sex abusers are in some way related to the child. The reality is that child sexual abusers no longer fit the profile of being homeless strangers loitering in parks, seducing children by passing out candy to an unwary child.

The Child Molestation Prevention Study (Abel & Harlow, 2001) profiles child *molesters* over the age of 25, as virtually indistinguishable from other American men with respect to religiosity, marital status and employment.

Interestingly, according to Jensen (2016) 5% of people in public schools have had issues with sexual molestation compared with 11% in church schools. This surprising fact may be accounted for by the naïveté of Christian school administrators in the past, however, with increased awareness it is expected that predators will no longer see parochial schools as being a gift.

Again, these findings may not be so surprising when a 2006 study, quoted by Jensen (2016) gathered data from 111 incarcerated S/Os who were classified according to their religious preferences as atheists, drop outs (those who had left their faith), converts (who had come to faith in prison) or stayers (those who practiced their faith before incarceration and remained "faithful"). Those who had the most convictions, more victims and younger victims were the stayers –perhaps because they had better connections with a community that had its head in the sand! Certainly church communities are not immune to sexual molestation.

A study of 652 child molesters in Minnesota determined how convicted S/Os were associated to their victims. Sixteen per cent were parents, 14% were step-parents, 15% were other types of relatives, 26% were family friends, 22% worked with kids at school, camps, sports et cetera, 22% we associated through church and only 5% were total strangers (Jensen, 2016). These figures show that step-parents who are perceived to be most at risk of molesting their step-child are not, in fact, a greater risk. Jensen explains this by stating that child sexual abuse is not relationship driven but behavior driven. A person who does not have a sex-drive directed towards children would never consider molesting a child, no matter what their relationship to the child was. Period.

PREVENTION AND PUNISHMENT

We have already mentioned that Jesus advocated a millstone to be hung around the neck of those we understand to be a child molester, and that they be thrown into the depths of the sea as punishment (Matthew 18:6). However, this punishment does not protect the child that was abused in the first place. Anyone who has molested a child deserves to be punished, but prevention is the key to avoiding the problem before the molestation occurs, before the child is afraid and emotionally injured.

Jail time and a life-long placement on the S/O registry may be an adequate punishment for some S/Os, but data about recidivism is difficult to obtain when S/Os are usually dishonest in their responses. "Recidivism" does not mean "re-offending" but rather "redetection" –being caught again. The reality is that law enforcement has no idea how many S/Os really do re-offend. According to Jensen (2016) a Canadian study followed S/Os 5, 10 and 20 years after release. At 20 years, 30-40% had been re-detected and 40-55% had committed more sexual offenses. But who is to really know? That is likely to be a conservative estimate knowing that S/Os are not honest. In times of stress, ordinary people, including S/Os, return to behaviors with which they are familiar and in time S/Os may get lackadaisical and let their guard down. Frequently child S/Os live for 50 years after being first caught and data collected three or five years after release can hardly show the truth about recidivism, especially when the data are selectively published, with bias, by persons often working with S/Os in the criminal justice system. According to Jensen (2016) who has worked all her professional life with S/Os, many will go 30-40 years without re-offending, according to them. Some though state that they re-offended once, only to change that information to having been re-detected once, but had actually re-offended fifty times. Truth can be elusive, but clearly there are many years in which S/Os may re-offend and be re-detected –or not.

Preventive medicine is a branch of medicine that works with patients who are at risk for specific diseases before the disease takes hold of them and ideally helps them avoid developing the disease. So pedophiles seeking help should be able to access mental health and medical treatment options that suit their condition, and so keep children safe *before* they act on their attraction. In doing this society will then be on its way to the *primary* prevention of child abuse, of being proactive, rather than reactive.

At present our society, and many others around the world, are frantically putting band-aids on a wound that is already festering. Society's fear that another child will be molested by a scary pedophile, drives MAPs further underground and accessing help more difficult. Because of this they may succumb to their inborn sexual desires or uncontrolled evil intent. In that instance, we can only institute *secondary* prevention as a child will have already been abused.

Christians are in the unique position of being available to listen to, or even support Level 1 pedophiles who are sexually attracted to children but choose not to act on that attraction. In so doing they will help to initiate the primary prevention for child sexual abuse and assist VPs in their effort to get professional help for this very specific condition. With growing awareness, the church can develop tools to be a support network to someone whose child, or spouse is predisposed towards pedophilia or to youth who are confused and frightened by their abnormal sexual urges as they venture into adult life. Christ's followers no longer need to turn their backs on society's Untouchables.

MAPs *are* the Untouchables of today and need to feel the Master's touch, as did the lepers of Jesus' time. Christians can take the first steps in giving hope to the hopeless, and

> Christ's followers no longer need to turn their backs on society's Untouchables.

friendship to those still shunned by society and who are seeking help to remain pure.

CHAPTER 5

PARADIGM SHIFT

The prevention of child sexual abuse (CSA) is on the verge of a major paradigm shift. Progress is slow but society is beginning to recognize that there are avenues to follow by both professionals, and the public, that can help to reduce CSA one child at a time.

Unfortunately, most people still fail to understand that learning about pedophilia and how to help pedophiles *will* prevent CSA. By no longer sweeping the topic of pedophilia under the carpet, they are taking the very *first* step in preventing CSA. Primary prevention happens *before* an incident occurs with the pain, ignominy, anger, fear (and more) that may ensue. Sweeping the topic under the carpet usually has exactly the opposite outcome from that intended as it sends pedophiles underground, devoid of support and more likely to act on their sexual drive. That being the case, the preventative measures that can be instituted can only be secondary measures because they are being instituted *after* a child has been molested.

Child molestation is wrong at every level although research shows that not every child who is molested will be emotionally or physically damaged in the long term. However, this does not mean that sexually molesting a child is okay and risk-free. The majority of

> **Children whose parents are divorced at 5-times more likely to be abused than children in intact families.**

children who are used sexually by an adult *are* affected adversely but can have fulfilling intimate relationships as adults, especially if they receive help from a qualified, effective counsellor.

RISK FACTORS

A child who is not loved by a parent is more susceptible to the unhealthy attention of another adult. Convicted S/Os admit that they look for the least challenging situations for them to operate in. Single parents' needs are great, they may be fragile and gullible and because of poverty their children may lack supervision. Child S/Os groom the parent of the type of child that appeals to their needs, each seeking specific characteristics in their favorite child. It might be a physical attribute like hair color, or a personality trait with some preferring gregarious children and others quiet. In developing a friendship with the parent, volunteering to help with child care or a birthday party, all the while increasing physical involvement with the child and making themselves indispensable to the parent, and available. They take their time, maybe a year or more, to set up the perfect, calculated relationship, and situations.

Children whose parents are divorced are 5-times more likely to be abused than children in intact families. This can be accounted for by the fact that these children live in two homes and have twice as many playmates and adults to interact with, thus exposing them to greater risk. The same applies if children attend multiple soccer camps or participate in a least two different churches' social activities. Associations are doubled and the risk increases.

CATEGORIZING CSA

CSA is an evolving definition. It is impossible to define it uniformly as it varies across disciplines, social systems, research and laws. Theoretically the number of substantiated cases of CSA declined by 58% between 1992 and 2008 (Tabachnick & Klein, 2011), but this does not necessarily indicate a decrease in actual incidents of abuse. The apparent decrease may be the result of changing classifications. Viewing pictures of clothed, or partially clothed children can be recognized as CSA in some data while others might limit the classification to include only viewing pictures of pornographic activity with children. Changing the upper age limit for inclusion of children in a category from 13, to 15 or 18 years old, also results in an apparent change in the incidence. Other factors affecting the data might come from the pressure imposed by counsellors in the 1980s for clients to dredge up false memories of childhood abuse, so increasing the apparent incidence. Counsellors were doing their job but were somewhat misinformed by today's standards where much greater care is taken with respect to past, forgotten incidents.

Another reason to question whether or not there is a real decrease in CSA incidence is that families report incidences less because they do not wish to be stigmatized. They have witnessed what has happened to other families and prefer not to report it. Additionally, the harsh sentences judges are required to impose on child sexual abusers in some jurisdictions, are considered excessive by the judges, and very costly, particularly when the perpetrators are often teenagers. For this reason deals are cut with lesser sentences being imposed, causing an apparent reduction in CSA cases.

INCIDENCES AND PREVENTION

CSA in boys under 18 years of age is quoted as being as infrequent as one in twenty boys, to as common as one in six. This compares with one in three or four, for girls. But many professionals accept CSA rates as being one in four girls and one in seven boys by their thirteenth birthday.

With a little more that 10% of CSA cases being reported to the authorities and more stringent reporting laws, the trend of not reporting cases is likely to persist, and even increase. But whatever the real figures are, we are confident that any single case of CSA is one too many.

It is clear that what is being done to prevent CSA today isn't working very well. There is a growing body of evidence showing that authorities are being reactive and not working towards the primary prevention of CSA. Too little is done to prevent it happening *before* a child is victimized. "Stranger danger" and the registry of convicted S/Os can distract our attention from the greatest danger which is at home, and mandatory reporting laws make it nearly impossible for people with pedophilia to seek help *prior* to offending. It would be more productive if help could be provided to MAPs before molestation happens and perhaps the educated Christian community could help to make this a reality.

No longer is CSA "out there" where it can be ignored by regular folk because it reaches into every community, school, children's club, family and church. Nor can the Christian community be paralyzed, hoping it will go away or become someone else's problem. Christians must become part of the solution.

Without being able to identify VPs, it is highly probable that church goers may be sitting next to one on their pew. By keeping MAPs away from help and hidden from view, myths about them are perpetuated and children remain at risk. Through ignorance people prolong the falsehood that pedophiles are Untouchables who are waiting for the first opportunity to molest kids. In ignorance they condemn MAPs (Level 1 and Level 2) indefinitely to a life of secrecy, fear and depression, while taking from them any hope of overcoming their propensities.

ACCESSING PROFESSIONAL HELP

VPs seeking assistance from mental health professionals (MHPs) may be unable to get a referral since there are few therapists trained, or willing to deal with this issue. Therapists providing help to VPs have often been mistreated by the professional community however, with the increasing knowledge of pedophilia and the specialized help pedophiles need, this critical attitude towards MHPs who are stepping up to help VPs is beginning to slowly lessen.

> Secondary stigmatization and its effects…in part account for 95% of MHPs not wishing to provide counseling to non-offending MAPs.

According to Jennifer Weeks, PhD who quotes a 2010 study from Germany that secondary stigmatization and its effects projected onto sympathetic therapists and their practices, in part accounts for 95% of MHPs not wishing to provide counseling to non-offending MAPs. Obviously this contributes to the difficulty experienced by non-offending pedophiles in finding experienced counsellors to help them. Treatment is rarely made available to pedophiles until they *have* molested a child. Such is their lot, at the cost of another child's safety.

Jason, a non-offending pedophile, was without hope. He knew his propensity and was terrified that he would eventually offend. "It is only a matter of time", he told himself. With nowhere to turn, he eventually disclosed his pedophilic attraction to a counsellor. Then instead of being given help, he lost his job, and his children were taken away from him. Jason is just one of many.

The general public expects professionals to help them when they are physically, emotionally or psychologically in need. Qualified marriage counsellors help people through a rocky marriage and provide tools to restore their marriages to beautiful, lasting relationship. Physicians are trained to diagnose and treat physical diseases and health educators and preventive medicine practitioners educate us in avoiding common lifestyle diseases. But who is willing to help the non-offending pedophile?

REPREHENSIBLE AND IRRESPONSIBLE

It is alarming that in January 2014 Walden University of Minneapolis, MN expelled a student from what Walden U boasts to be an excellent graduate counseling program. Walden U's web site and handbook profess a non-discriminatory policy towards students with respect to sexual orientation, religion, race etc.

At the start of the on-line program, a VP declared his desire to counsel MAPs (along with all other clients) but found the faculty incompetent in this aspect of counseling and holding a negative attitude towards his participation. This might have been from the obvious ignorance of the faculty, but in expelling the student their near-sightedness lost them a golden opportunity to join the few universities who acknowledge this paradigm shift to reducing CSA, by training competent counsellors for the non-offending pedophilic population.

It was not until the student had almost completed his studies that Walden University dismissed him from the program based on his sexual orientation. Walden U did not carry through on their initial offer of specialized counseling nor give him any recourse. Later he lost his case against the university for unlawful dismissal from the program on a technicality, because their non-discriminatory disclaimer *did not, in reality*, create a contract. The university pocketed the hefty fees for an almost completed graduate degree and showed themselves to be non-progressive in their counseling program, by refusing to train even one clinician focused on helping the pedophilic population.

A number of Walden University's counseling department faculty are openly gay and yet curiously, Walden U *insists* that all counseling students learn to provide LGBT affirmative therapy even though the faculty considered LGBT issues as "normal" behaviors and not requiring treatment! It is baffling that they provide counsellors for this "healthy" community of people, while being unprepared, and unwilling to train counsellors for MAPs who are seeking competent counsellors to reduce the incidence of CSA! Hopefully Walden University will learn from their errors.

GOD OVER-RULES

The devil may try to thwart those working towards providing assistance to vulnerable MAPs, but with his knowledge about the treatment of pedophiles, the former student was in a unique position to consult with VPs on-line anonymously without them being fearful of being turned over to the authorities, as he is not a mandatory reporter. This led to the birth of a new ministry for VPs. God turned Satan's contrived plans into a blessing.

Slowly the number of counsellors willing to

provide support and guidance to non-offending MAPs is growing, even though they may not boldly advertise their services. Treating VPs can place counsellors in extremely difficult positions where the application of laws requiring them to report incidents of viewing pornographic materials or sexually interacting with a prepubescent child in years past, may not now be the best action for the client. Reporting this could ruin the relationship that an older, non-offending pedophile is building with a counsellor (Clark-Fory, May 2016). Clark-Fory concludes with, "The question is whether the law strikes a good enough balance between protecting kids and keeping the door open for those in need of help—from the minor-attracted uncle who has vowed not to touch his niece to the teenage boy who has looked at child porn, to the sex abuse survivor who doesn't want her case reported." These are hard questions to answer but as reputable universities begin to provide education supporting this population and investigative reporters (Tourjee, 2016; VarmitCoyote, 2013), photojournalists like Alex McBride Wilson (2016) and other interested parties (Lopez, 2016) delve into the nuances of the law and keeping children safe. Counsellors and MHPs will be given opportunities to learn how to treat

Level 1 pedophiles, and those who have offended in the past, and who wish to build a clean slate and receive help (Level 2).

The laws regarding mandatory reporting need to be revisited because they do not appear to be bringing about the anticipated outcome. Our nation, and others, are so determined to protect children by reporting any suspicion of child endangerment,

> Our nation, and others, are so determined to protect children by reporting any suspicion of child endangerment, that it has backfired.

that it has backfired. Now it is time to educate the public and review laws so that the primary prevention of CSA will be a recognized as a viable treatment modality for pedophiles seeking treatment. The present system is broken, and those wanting, or needing help, are prohibited from getting it before a child is abused.

New research data and knowledge about MAPs are resulting in successful treatment options that can be matched to each pedophile's specific need. Knowing the possible risks *before* a situation arises, allows preventive action to be instituted early and we are beginning to recognize that the early professional management of MAPs decreases the incidence of CSA.

CHAPTER 6

ON-LINE SUPPORT GROUPS

As with other minority groups who need a voice and are being ignored, or people who have rare diseases with few cases spanning across continents, the Internet provides that voice, knowledge, resources and support. For pedophiles, on-line support groups consist of an anonymous network of counsellors, professionals, VPs who want to help others in their journey while seeking support for themselves, young MAPs with a million questions, family members with a need to know, and the occasional child sex-offender who has done time, received treatment and is determined to maintain a VP status from henceforth.

These on-line support groups allow members to discuss a multitude of ideas specific to the group. This may be to encourage newly emerging pedophiles to ask questions that bother them and for which they have no answer, to understand better their attraction and to no longer be isolated in a world that does not understand pedophilia. Nothing related to pedophilia is off-limits, which of itself is healing to the formerly isolated pedophile. However the moderators are careful to allow only posts that support their site's mission and assist participants through a bewildering life journey.

VirPed, B4U-ACT, ASAPinternational, StopSO etc

The fastest growing on-line peer support group for pedophiles is VirPed.org (Virtuous Pedophiles) which emerged in June 2012. VirPed takes a strong stand against any sexual contact between an adult and a child and as of June 2016 has more than 1600 members. Due to hysteria that is often manifested even against those who have never acted on their sexual attraction to children, nearly all of the participants use pseudonyms. Their comments provide valuable insight into the life experiences of people with pedophilia who choose not to act on their attraction to children. Most of the contributors are from the United

States of America but by Spring 2016 nearly 30 nations were represented including the UK, Russia and Iran with an increasing number of females participating in the forum, as well as family members of people with pedophilia.

The members of a second on-line support group are at B4U-ACT. This group refer to pedophiles as minor-attracted persons (MAPs), whereas the VirPed group choose to use the nomenclature "virtuous pedophile" to indicate their choice to never offend. Annual workshops are organized by B4U-Act to bring their message to members, counsellors and others involved in being active in promoting their message.

A third on-line site is ASAPinternational.org (the Association for Sexual Abuse Prevention) which bases its content on three core values: 1) An adult should never sexually interact with children; 2) People with pedophilia do not choose to be attracted to children, but they can choose not to act on that attraction; and 3) Therapy does not change a person's sexual orientation, but it can help the person accept his or her attraction to children without acting on it.

ASAP, VirPed and B4U-Act treat all participants with respect, recognizing pedophiles as regular people with specific needs, not as monsters or ticking time-bombs. Confidentiality is vital to every therapeutic relationship whether on line or in person.

ASAP clearly upholds the truth about pedophilia that *attraction is not the same as action* and while ASAP cannot "cure" the attraction, it provides information to assist pedophiles in dealing with their sexuality and connects VPs with counsellors who practice near the VP's home whether in the US or elsewhere. A growing list of mental health professionals who are willing to work with non-offending

> ASAPinternational.org connects VPs with counsellors who practice near the VP's home in the US or elsewhere.

pedophiles is listed on the web site. These all support the primary prevention of CSA. People contacting ASAPinternational can also speak with a live person by phone. Headed by a Christian whose goal is not to push his Christian beliefs on the caller, ASAP will interact and pray with callers if they desire. Its ministry is for the pedophilic population. ASAP workshops are held for members, MHPs, counsellors in training, faculty and interested parties wherever sufficient numbers will gather anywhere in the world.

For Christians who recognize the commitment of

marriage as being between a man and a woman as instituted in Eden, one situation arises that results in a less than perfect solution in a less than perfect world. On a few occasions ASAP has recommended that an unmarried male pedophile whose primary sexual attraction is towards prepubescent boys should enter a homosexual relationship with a consenting adult male, rather than molest a child. Just as sanctification, the process of being made-over into Christ's likeness through the power of the Holy Spirit can take a life-time, so moving away from interacting sexually with a child, towards the less harmful behavior of interacting sexually with a consenting adult of the same gender could be the first step towards upward change. MAPs who accept the Holy Spirit's working in their life can be changed over time so that their former pedophilic and homosexual desires will no longer control them.

Ana, an on-line contributor describes her adult sexual attraction as heterosexual, while she is also attracted to young girls. Others report that their attraction to children comes and goes, or may only be present for certain children regardless of their age and gender. This is mystifying, but nothing is impossible for God (Luke 1:37) who will work to better *all* situations.

StopSO (Specialist Treatment Organisation for the Prevention of Sexual Offending) (2016) is an organization based in the UK. It is a nationwide network of treatment providers who work with anyone who is worried about their sexual behavior and feels that they may be at risk of sexually offending or re-offending. StopSO provides support to the families of those who have committed a sexual offence, training workshops for MHPs and referrals.

Curiosity is mounting about pedophilia and MHPs, social science researchers and interested individuals worldwide are producing documentaries to educate the public and pedophiles. Todd, a recognized VP, has been out for more than a decade and recently told his story on several media venues with very encouraging responses (Upadhye, 2016). Other documentaries are in the pipeline.

PEDOPHILIA IS NOT A DISEASE

How a person chooses to refer to themselves may be of no consequence to some, however it is no longer acceptable to call a person who has epilepsy "an epileptic", so this matter should be briefly addressed. People with a pedophilic orientation may not be concerned about being called "a pedophile" or "a minor-attracted person" because it is their orientation and not a disease. However, in saying that they *have* pedophilia, implies that pedophilia is a disease. Similarly, homosexuals often refer to themselves as being "gay" or "lesbian", describing their sexual orientation, and not a disease.

COMING OUT OF THE TOY-BOX EXPERIENCES

The founders of VirPed do not encourage people with pedophilia to come out of the toy-box, but many VPs find it a very liberating experience to acknowledge to someone that they are sexually attracted to children. This single act usually decreases their likelihood of acting on their desire although there can be a negative back-lash. Most VPs though describe the experience as positive as long as their confidante realizes the *difference between attraction and action*. The following on-line comments were posted anonymously about coming out.

Allan shared his experience when he outed himself after being on an emergency hold for suicidal ideation, "At the state hospital I was told I belong in prison and that if I did kill myself, I would be doing society a favor. The greatest part about being told this is that it was by a patient advocate. Yep, the guy who is hired to make sure my rights aren't violated."

Bjorn described the trauma he experienced in

coming out. "I was super stressed due to changing my medications and feeling like I might act out on some of my urges towards children. I naively went to the mental health place at the hospital and told them what I was worried about. When I first showed up they were friendly and seemed like they wanted to help. All they did was call the police and offer absolutely zero support."

Chad wrote, "I just came out a couple of days ago to one friend. She's been completely accepting and I've told her everything. She's read every one of my threads on VirPed. She's talked to the pedos (pedophiles) I talk to on kik (app connecting friends; parents beware). I've given her every reason to think poorly of me and have been constantly asking her how she's feeling or if anything has changed. Nothing has changed. Sure I've been avoiding eye contact. Yes, it's awkward at times. Of course I'm looking for things to blow up in my face. But they haven't, and she's insistent that it won't." Eventually his friend started posting on VirPed as well.

Don also had a positive experience coming out. "It is definitely weird. I also thought I wouldn't be able to look my wife in the eye from the moment she knew, but thankfully it hasn't happened. You're the exact same person you were the minute before they knew about it, and ultimately that carries more weight. I guess it depends on the person you tell, how close you are and how frequently you interact."

Elton described coming out to his wife when he was falsely accused by a foster girl who had been in their home three years earlier. "I assured her I did not do what the girl had alleged, but that in fact I was sexually attracted to little girls. In the next few years, I came out to my sisters, my daughters, other relatives, dozens of friends and the general public. It can be awkward at first but gets easier every time. I have never had a negative reaction from people who understand that I choose not to act on my attraction to children. My wife occasionally brings up the subject, but does not want to talk about it most of the time. Sometimes she just needs assurance that I love her more than any little girl."

Frank said, "My wife knows, and let's just say that it is awkward. I pretty much never refer to the attraction and have never specified the age of boys which interest me. Luckily, we just talk about me going to my therapist and meetings and whatever, and that is still awkward."

Gareth added, "I have come out to more than a

dozen friends since I realized my attraction, but it never really got any easier over time. It is a touchy subject, and there is no way to predict how the person will react. You are in essence painting a huge target on yourself and hoping the other person will not take the shot, so to say. I still am very 'sensitive' when it comes to discussing these attractions, and looking back I wonder how I had the courage to keep on coming out again and again."

HELP FOR TEENS?

Although the on-line sites are for adults, occasionally teens access them. They may be living with their parents and confused by being sexually attracted to prepubescent children, and seek help. One such 15 year-old sought intermediary support by asking ASAP to talk to his family about his sexual attraction, and another attended a conference to learn more. The trials faced by these teens cannot be compared with the confusion same-sex attraction youth face for although homosexual desires may be met with hostility and even horror, this is rarely now the case in western society. Being disowned by parents is a justified fear of young MAPs who may not have the language to describe their attraction. They are assumed to be evil perverts from the get-go, and told so, and parents are often blind-sided by the revelation. However, more parents are in the know, and calling for help.

Christians hold to a fundamental belief that everyone is tainted by sin and that many have sexual urges and behaviors that do not hold to the standards set out in the Bible. But pedophilia? That is a completely different situation for which most have no answer and initially exhibit the usual disgust. How can they know when no one discusses the problem?

PARTNERS AND PARENTS' PROBLEMS

Some contributors to the sites are spouses or girl-friends, husbands or boy-friends of pedophiles, or parents of young MAPs. After partners off-load onto them the truth about their sexual orientation, the partner finds themselves in a new role. This is not without challenges too. They did not chose to be married to, or in a stable relationship with, a pedophile. It is likely a shocking and unwanted situation. This could negatively affect the dynamics of an intimate relationship. Salvaging the relationship, or building a better, stronger one can be challenging.

If the spouse/girl-friend is female and he is attracted to little girls, she now not only has to compete with unattainable beauty portrayed in airbrushed female perfection as seen on media, but also with cute little girls. If he is attracted to little boys, then that conjures up concerns related to bi-sexuality. Each one has to deal with a mound of confusion. Justifiably each may wonder to where their partner's mind wanders during sexual intimacy.

Knowing that a partner is a pedophile adds concerns about CSA when there are young children in the household fitting the preferred age/gender of the pedophilic partner. Dealing with this aspect of the family, or bringing children into a previously childless relationship, can be daunting. How should a partner deal with this new information?

Similarly, where can a parent turn when they learn that their child is not "normal" and is sexually attracted to young children? If they reveal this information to a mandatory reporter, or seek information about pedophilia from the wrong person, their home may never be the same again. Their child might be removed from them and branded (incorrectly) a child molester. They may be ostracized by their extended family, and even their church may turn their back on them when they get wind of the situation. Such can be the quandary of partners and parents.

VirPed, ASAPinternational, B4U-Act forums and other blogs give guidance and support to MAPs and their partners (or parents) who are seeking help. In time, hopefully, the Christian community will have a role to play in helping VPs as they struggle with their sexual identification.

Beverly wrote, "When he told me, it was a lot to take in, but ultimately, I knew my best friend had been struggling and I just wanted to be there. I hugged him way more than he probably would have liked. I had read about some things on pedophilia earlier this year and that personally helped me a lot. He and I have always been really honest with each other, so I just told him to share with me whenever and whatever he feels like. This is completely new to both of us, so there are awkward times just as he said, but I think it's only going to get better as he realizes I will support him until the end of time and I learn a bit more. Our friendship is not going to change because of something that's not in his control."

KEEPING CHILDREN SAFE

VPs are committed to keeping children safe. Many are confident they will never molest a child while others put strategies in place to avoid a slip-up. A number of threads on VirPed.org deal with keeping children safe from a completely different perspective than would be discussed by the general public. Such open discussions might even horrify the public.

Hal asked, "Why is that such a strong theme here in the sense/idea that pedophiles have a harder time controlling themselves?" to which Inman responded, "I think a lot of people here have internalized the idea that pedophiles are a ticking time-bomb. I've noticed that pretty much everyone who is totally comfortable with pedophilia seems completely sure that they're not going to offend, and the people who are most uncomfortable with pedophilia are the most worried about it." Josh observed, "I don't think one can be a truly conscientious virtuous pedophile without occasionally questioning one's ability to refrain.... *You can never let your guard down.* This is the reason why I have made the deliberate decision to just not be around kids at all, even though I am certain of my ability to control myself. I need to feel doubly sure that I will be fine –and moreover, that I will not have any horrible crushes on any kid."

Keith added, "Sexuality cannot always be fully

controlled when you're aroused, so certain patterns of behavior and thoughts can help to find out if you're on the way to getting too close or too aroused, to handle things reasonably and responsibly... So basically it is about strategies to:

1. Stay calm and don't act weird around kids.
2. Recognize situations that would lead you personally onto a slippery slope.
3. Don't get lost in screwed up thought patterns to convince yourself that the child wants 'more' from you.
4. Find ways to live with your personal sexual preference and pattern of arousal without acting irresponsibly and maintain happiness in life."

Liam wrote, "One thing I always had was the desire and determination to never do anything to make a child uncomfortable. But in my late teens I did some things that made me uncomfortable. So that got added to the list of things to avoid.... My point is that in 45 years, I've never succumbed to 'urges'. I'm quite confident that it would be impossible."

In approximately 30% of cases of child sexual abuse, alcohol is involved however drug use, especially methamphetamines, is becoming a greater problem. Molesters act out a behavior they already have in their life with less conscience, not a new behavior not previously acted upon (Jensen, 2016).

Mart realized how alcohol can affect actions. "It was important for me to carefully limit my alcohol intake when I am in a situation where there is a possibility I will be spending time with a child 'alone.' Adults do crazy things with each other when drunk, and can become especially flirtatious, sexually pushy, etc. when they are attracted to another person. This behavior is sometimes problematic in adults, and is surely even more risky between an adult and a child."

Neil admits, "I know out of experience that my judgement and impulse control are impaired if I have a crush on someone.... When my feelings are directed towards a child, I need to think several steps ahead so I don't risk putting myself in a position where it seems sensible to me (then and there) to explain anything about how I feel. For me, keeping children safe is focused on preventing myself from ever letting them know that my feelings for them are out of the ordinary."

In reading these comments we see sincere people who have insight into their problem and do not wish to commit CSA. On-line support sites provide grass-root assistance and discussion opportunities to all participants from the newest member to established participants. Frequently such sites are the very first help the new participant has been able to access. The responses, and their participation, can give them a glimmer of hope in a formerly dark, dark world.

> On-line support sites provide grass-root assistance and discussion opportunities to all participants. Frequently such sites are the very first help the new participant has been able to access.

Other threads deal with matters of masturbation, fantasizing about children, child pornography, VPs working with children, marriage and having a family, accepting oneself as a MAP, dealing therapeutically with feelings of guilt, shame, and anxiety, the educated use of language applied to pedophilia, the role of professional treatment, if it can be obtained, to help individuals manage any potential risk of sexually interacting with a child –and much more.

CHAPTER 7

TREATING PEDOPHILES

Recent documentaries show how it is virtually impossible for a VP to access professional help. The cards are stacked high against success, because at present almost everyone equates "pedophile" with "child molester". Most people will have a hard time processing the fact that these terms are not interchangeable.

Three viewpoints as to how to treat pedophiles might be a variation on: 1) put them all in jail –and never let them out; 2) encourage them to commit suicide because they are a waste of space; or 3) address pedophilia in a meaningful way even though it is hopeless. None of these options produces an iota of comfort to a pedophile.

A variety of professionals refer to three levels of sexuality in pedophilia simply as attraction, arousal and action. The Dunkelfeld manual refers to them as self-concept, fantasies and behaviors (Beier, 2013), while Seto (2016) describes these levels as "sexual attention, sexual response and sexual behavior".

What is clear is that generally the public continues to believe that every pedophile is a monster, and as such, cannot be trusted. Eventually they will molest children if given the opportunity. Research shows this is not the case, but often it is not until a person finds out that someone they know, respect or love is actually a pedophile, that their reasoning is challenged. Then pedophilia becomes personal, taking on new dimensions to which real answers must be found.

The Christian community is in a position to assist this maligned population. Being a disciple of Christ puts an onus on His followers to treat MAPs with compassion because like everyone else, they are God's children. It behooves them to become informed, as should their church family, and society at large. When a basic informed understanding develops, society will begin to recognize the unfair hand being dealt to pedophiles and the complexities

VPs face.

PEDOPHILIA IS NOT A CHOICE

No one chooses to be a pedophile. No one wakes up one morning and says, "I think I'll become a pedophile today." This is ridiculous. But ever since Eve and Adam fell prey to Satan's lies, mankind has inherited a sinful nature. That fallen nature may be a desire to act on a same-sex orientation, or a pedophilic orientation, or to act selfishly, commit adultery, steal, or "covet (desire) your neighbor's house… your neighbor's wife, his manservant or maidservant, his ox or his donkey, or anything that belongs to your neighbor (Exodus 20:17)." Who better than Christians to lend a helping hand to a fellow traveler because they understand the contagious effect of sin, and know that overcoming anyone's sinful desires can be only over a life time by the grace of God? This process is called "sanctification" – the work of a lifetime.

In whatever manner pedophilia comes about, it manifests itself as a sexual orientation. This terminology can upset those who do not wish it to be aligned with other sexual orientations, such as homosexuality. Others might label it as a dangerous and aberrant orientation, but there is no known statistical correlation between it and autistic spectrum diseases, although people on the spectrum have their own unique challenges in building and maintaining relationships.

No single treatment methodology will cure pedophiles of pedophilia. Pedophilia is a life-long journey in which pedophiles must learn how to avoid acting on their

> **Pedophilia is a life-long journey in which pedophiles must learn how to avoid acting on their attraction.**

attraction. Having an attraction, or desire, is not sinful. It is human. But not taking the next step into action is always preferable, especially for pedophiles whose actions can negatively impact a child for life. No pedophile wishes to be sent to prison, with all that entails for them and their loved ones, however it appears that some jurisdictions are intent on punishing even thought-crime.

SEEKING PROFESSIONAL HELP

The following anonymous comments from the internet have been included to provide a cursory view of the very real challenges MAPs face when navigating their world when seeking help from an MHP. Seeking psychological help might be one of the earliest challenges, although some VPs were fortunate.

Oscar reported a very positive experience. "I've

been having meetings once a week with a psychiatrist. She doesn't have much experience with MAPs, a few have come in before (after going through the legal system), but I'm the first she's met with who hasn't been arrested. Even though she's an old woman, she is very compassionate towards my plight, and even though she doesn't know how to help me (something I don't even know), she's been listening to me. She says I need to become friends with that part of me that wants to do bad things and doesn't encourage any shame for my desires."

Poddar wrote, "I've been seeing a therapist for about two years now. I went because I was really depressed, but I told him about my attraction to, and fantasies about, young teen boys almost immediately. We talk a lot about fantasies and dreams and about how I relate to other people. It's a safe place to talk to an actual human being in person, so I'm glad I decided to tell him."

Quincy also had a positive experience. "I first went into therapy when I was 18 years old. It saved my life at the time. Sure, it didn't 'fix' me, but it did help me to survive one of the most trying times of my entire life. I was out to my therapist about being a pedophile and that was the main focus of our sessions. Back then, I was even very open with him about the children in my life who I was friends with, and he was cool about it."

Carolina wrote, "I've not had very good luck when it comes to therapy. My first one outed me; the next two made me feel like a sociopath. I even had one tell me that I was faking my attractions and only men suffer from pedophilia." Carolina sought help while she was in the air force and when the therapist outed her, she was stigmatized as a criminal and discharged even though she had not had any sexual contact with a child.

Raj reported, "The first therapist I had immediately contacted Child Protective Services. They proceeded to contact all my friends and family who had prepubescent girls, which led to me being ostracized. This eventually led to a suicide attempt which almost succeeded."

Seamus wrote, "I've had so many bad experiences with MHPs that I'm not sure I trust them. I have come across people who tried to pretend that minor attraction does not exist. According to them, I am not a reliable witness of my own sexuality. According to them, I am too intelligent, too good looking, and too socially competent to be minor attracted. According to them, I am also confused; I am not minor attracted, I only think that I am."

Thom added, "I would absolutely say that it is incredibly important that therapists understand our perspective. Dealing with a court appointed 'therapist' was one of the worst things that has ever happened to me. He was insulting and blamed me for my attraction. He told me that I would 'most likely offend on someone.' That isn't okay, not for a therapist to say. I would say reach out to those people. There are thousands of S/Os going home after therapy sessions and contemplating suicide like I was."

Ulysses wrote, "My pedophilia came to the forefront again when my marriage of 25 years ended. I went to a counsellor to deal with other issues, but when I mentioned my attraction to little girls I was promptly abandoned without a referral. As a result, I felt hopeless, sure that I would inevitably offend."

> "When I mentioned my attraction to little girls I was promptly abandoned without a referral."

With these comments in mind it is easy to understand the situation young, and older pedophiles find themselves in. No one wants to be Untouchable, nor ostracized. For someone already distressed at finding themselves dealing with a sexuality issue that is a taboo topic, they may not have the vocabulary to discuss their sexuality proficiently with professionals, let alone with acquaintances or friends.

By introducing the topic of pedophilia to people not educated in the realities of pedophilia, VPs often find themselves cast further out of society than they perceived themselves as already being. This can lead to devastating

> **By introducing the topic of pedophilia to people not educated in the realities of pedophilia, virtuous pedophiles often find themselves cast further out of society than they perceived themselves as already being.**

consequences and requires VPs to decide whether the hope of finding real help exceeds the risk of being further hated.

TREATMENT OPTIONS

Family physicians and psychiatrists use a variety of modalities to treat pedophiles today. While they recognize that they are unable to rid pedophiles of pedophilia, health care practitioners use treatments to decrease the likelihood that the client will act on their sexual urges. This may include testosterone-reducing drugs or anti-depressants that are known to decrease sex drive. Most patients will already have a degree of depression by the time they seek treatment so medications need to be prescribed carefully and monitored for unsafe side effects.

Castration remains a controversial option. Many state justice systems view it as the ultimate cure and at least one state pays for the castration of criminal pedophiles even though some castrated men have managed to reoffend. For this reason, most physicians prefer medical hormone suppression since they can monitor this treatment over time (Palmer, 2010).

INDIVIDUAL AND GROUP THERAPY

Counsellors working individually with non-offending pedophiles may use client-centered therapy which builds trust and rapport between the client and the therapist, who will further use mindfulness-based cognitive therapy. This will enhance their self-confidence and belief in themselves as being their own agent and in control of themselves. In separating the person from the problem, pedophilia no longer defines them and they can start to understand pedophilia as a behavior that can be defeated. By working with the therapist as a team member, they can look at specific situations where what could have been a situation where the desire to molest a child was overwhelming, was resisted. In discussing what happened in such situations, mindfulness can convert what was a saving behavior into techniques that can be applied to other situations. In using cognitive behavioural therapy, the counsellor can zero in on the client's thoughts, identify what might be problem thoughts and replace them with behavior changing thoughts.

According to one therapist, "Society's treatment of pedophiles, particularly in Australia, is extreme and self-defeating. They are demonised and ostracised. Some people who are generally opposed to the death penalty, want it re-introduced for pedophiles. It does not matter the offence, kill them all. Many clients are very afraid of being discovered, so overcoming this fear is a significant part of early treatment. There must be many others who are too afraid to seek treatment at all, so the extreme societal attitude is an obstruction to treatment."

> **Pedophiles are demonised and ostracised. Some people who are generally opposed to the death penalty, want it re-introduced for pedophiles.**

In cases of molestation within the home, family therapy is often recommended as a prelude to heavily supervised father-child (or mother-child) visits. Some clients eventually get to see their children alone. Others may not.

In some group therapy situations, participants discuss the nature and frequency of their sexual fantasies from a level footing, as well as everyday life stresses that increase their chances of acting on their attraction. They are taught to empathize with past and potential victims and encouraged to interact healthfully with peers which, in their shame and guilt, they may have avoided in the past. Kenneth Quinn (2015), formerly a licensed counsellor, in *Mind of a Molester* carries the reader through different therapies that he experienced as a pedophile and later as an adjudicated child molester. Group therapy he saw as "one important means of working on thinking errors, receiving feedback and facing confrontation when appropriate (p87)."

Quinn supported participation in Sex Addicts Anonymous (SAA) although MHPs are not in agreement that acting-out on pedophilic attraction is an addiction. Others see child molestation as being the result of childhood behaviors and use transactional approaches. Whatever may be the source of the behaviour, Quinn sees the 12-steps of SAA as providing an excellent tool for stopping harmful behavior and dealing with temptations. "I believe that all of these approaches can be combined into an effective group of alternative approaches...My research and experience demonstrate that S/Os are a very diverse group and not all approaches will work for everyone. Treatment must be tailored to the individual." Quinn lists three essential elements necessary for change to happen: 1) a desire for change, 2) a belief that change is possible, 3) a belief that they are worthy of change despite their past (p.61).

CHILD PORNOGRAPHY?

On-line discussions show that many contributors are ignorant of what constitutes child pornography, but so is the general public and the laws about it are not static. The regulations imposed by states vary considerably. Some states recognize regular, family pictures of clothed children playing together as child pornography if viewed in association with higher levels of child pornography. In some

> It is an immovable, undeniable fact that children *cannot* consent to sexual behavior with adults.

jurisdictions hentai, computer generated (virtual) drawings of children are considered child pornography if the drawings *look like* a child, even though they are not real children. Forensic psychologist Luke Broomhall prefers to use the term "sexual exploitation material" instead of "child pornography" because pornography is really "recorded sexual acts between consenting adults" which makes it a misnomer. Broomhall (2016) states that no matter what may be the causative factors that result in pedophiles interacting sexually with a child, it is an immovable, undeniable fact that children *cannot* consent to sexual behavior with adults. Adults therefore have a legal and moral obligation to control their sexual impulses.

A very destructive behavior of child S/Os, and some non-offending pedophiles, can be leaving child sexual exploitation material "accidently" on a laptop to gauge children's attraction to such material and can get them interested in sexual behaviors. It is quoted that 55-85% of S/Os view sexual

> **Exposure to digital pornography is toxic to human sexual health at every age.**

exploitation material. The latter figure was confirmed by polygraph and the former number by confession, according to Cory Jewell Jensen (2016). Children watching porn with an adult can be more easily blackmailed into not reporting the experience (or more advanced sexual behaviors), however there is a 97% conviction rate for child pornography if it is reported since the evidence is on hand. Exposure to digital pornography is toxic to human sexual health at every age, not just in childhood. Anecdotally Christian men have a greater problem with digital pornography than do non-Christian men.

FANTASIES AND MASTURBATION

Some counsellors will advise clients to cease contact with friends who have children of a vulnerable age and to work towards gradually increasing the age of the subjects of their sexual fantasies. Developing healthy sexual relationships with an adult, or even frequent masturbation, may reduce libido and reduce the incidence of sexual interactions with a child. It can help them *not* to sexually abuse a child and some MAPs use it as a release valve to reduce the risk of acting out with a real child. However, others are categorially against masturbation in any form, as for them it increases the likelihood of CSA.

Other old-fashioned treatments such as covert sensitization and aversive conditioning may be recommended. However, large-scale studies of recidivism suggest that they have little effect on pedophilic behavior in the real world.

DUNKELFELD PROJECT

In Germany, mandatory reporting laws differ from those in the US and people with pedophilia can seek confidential help without fear of imprisonment. The Dunkelfeld Project (2015), provides group counseling to pedophiles seeking help *before* they act on their attraction. According to forensic psychologist Luke Broomhall (2016) more than 425 individuals have successfully completed the program, and more than ten times that number of enquiries have been made. There is a long waiting list to get into the program. Health care practitioners are likely to recommend counselling in group therapy (if available) as part of a treatment regimen.

RELATIONSHIPS

Developing relationships with peers and having a same-age sexual partner Broomhall (2016) says could be helpful to young pedophiles however, when they are not able to speak openly about

> Early intervention, before young pedophiles act on their attraction, will decrease the incidence of child sexual abuse.

pedophilia, and when ideas and conversations are blocked, adverse outcomes follow. Broomhall believes that early intervention, before young pedophiles act on their attraction, will decrease the incidence of CSA.

Broomhall further reminds his audience that pedophilia has a broad spectrum extending from the callous pervert who engages in sex with a child as often as he can with no concern for the child's well-being, to the pedophile who has never touched or violated a child, but who may possess sexual exploitation material of children under 13 years old on his computer. Sadly, when false accusations are made about CSA, and later recognized as such, the non-offending pedophile's life has usually been ruined. Pedophiles are not

> **Pedophiles are not innocent until proven guilty. They are always guilty –even if later found innocent by the court.**

innocent until proven guilty. They are always guilty –even if later found innocent by the court.

NO SINGLE TREATMENT OPTION

Cantor & McPhail (2016) recognize that one treatment modality cannot fit all VPs and therefore, for some VPs, being in "social relationships with children (e.g. friendships and coaching)" was "more satisfying than the possibility of having a sexual relationship with a child." They further point out that if some VPs are denied social relationships with children, they may become more fixated on, and troubled by, their attraction.

For many years James Cantor PhD, CPsych at the University of Toronto (Faculty of Medicine) has been a strong voice in getting the truth about pedophilia out to professionals and lay people alike. He has researched pedophilia using fMRIs and acknowledges the difficulties in treating non-offending pedophiles as being complex, but *not* insurmountable. He encourages clinicians and researchers to get involved in this "most challenging and open frontier."

In exploring these topics openly, it is clear that there is no "one-size-fits-all" treatment plan or methodology for pedophilia but as the Christian community begins to understand pedophilia, it could be part of

> **Clinicians and researchers should get involved in this "most challenging and open frontier."**

treatment options that will bring healing to the VP population, and protect children.

CHAPTER 8

PROTECTING OUR CHILDREN

Children are vulnerable and are no match for the psychopathic, criminal, antisocial child molester who appears to be nothing but a charming, well spoken, helpful and valued member of the community. Such people *do* prey on children who they believe are an easy target.

Parents' circumstances can make it difficult for them to be fully involved in parenting their children at all times, and the offer of assistance can appear to be a blessing. Parents may be single, or have complex lives that pull them away from home, leaving their children to fend for themselves at times, to be dropped-off at church by one friend and picked up by others. Without a parent's healthy, warm affection children become even more vulnerable.

At one time child molesters may have been non-offending pedophiles although, as we discussed earlier, a non-offending pedophile may never become a child molester and not all child molesters are pedophiles but, for the purposes of this chapter we will examine how children can be protected by their parents and caring individuals from child molestation.

Child safety is a priority and today we know much about protecting our children than was not common knowledge even 10-years ago. Parents and the Christian community need to avail themselves of this knowledge. They can no longer be naïve and hide their head in the sand preferring to believe that churches are filled with saints, and therefore free of molestation. This just isn't so –and the financial outlays made by church organizations, along with verified stories of molestation, prove it. Children are more likely to be sexually abused at church and in church-related activities, at sports practices, in school or at friends' homes, than they are to be by the two or three convicted sex-offenders their parents know who live in their community. For this reason, parents must be attentive, informed, and keep their guard up -whilst not being paranoid.

CONTRACTS AND CHAPERONES IN CHURCH

Congregations should implement policies to protect children that are developed by higher levels of administration or developed independently in cooperation with counsellors, CPS and local law enforcement. The safety plans should require mandatory reporting of any suspicion of abuse by staff.

Some congregations develop a child protection plan that allows convicted S/Os to attend church but they are always required to be shadowed by a deacon or church elder. Other observation policies may be an Open Door Policy which requires a single adult never to be closeted in a room with a child, behind closed doors. If a door has a viewing window, it may be closed. Additionally, a No Child Left Alone Policy prevents a child being left alone with an adult when a parent/guardian is late to pick up the child after an activity. These policies not only protect children, but also decrease the likelihood of false accusations being made against a volunteer. Allegations negatively affect the church's impact in the community, whether or not there is any substance to them. These policies should be implemented *before* anything happens to a single child.

Although the pastor and a select few church leaders may be aware of the full story behind allowing a convicted S/O attend the church, by instituting the required chaperoning plan and a written contract for each S/O, they also assist the S/O should anything happen in the church when he is present. He can be free of suspicion because he is chaperoned all the time. Being chaperoned allows him to attend church without fear, while keeping children safe in his presence.

BEING ATTENTIVE AND ALERT

S/Os target children who are at risk. They know the profile and pay attention. Child molesters notice the super-touchy child who may like back rubs or sitting on adults' laps. They are watching.

Once a child has been sexually abused, they are 3-6% more likely to be abused again compared with children who have not been abused before, because their boundaries have been dulled and their understanding of sexuality has been distorted.

All parents need to be observant of behaviors that

are suspicious, just as would-be child molesters watch behaviors. Bank tellers are not well versed in the many counterfeit bills that are manufactured, but they know their own currency so well that

> **All parents need to be observant of behaviors that are suspicious, just as would-be child molesters watch behaviors.**

their attention is automatically tweaked when counterfeit bills pass before them.

According to Jensen (2016), the litmus test for recognizing concerning behavior being done to someone else is to ask ourselves the question "Would I do that?" If the answer is "No", then further investigation is warranted.

Jensen has worked with convicted S/Os for many years and therefore has insight into the way S/Os think and act. They are careful observers of behavior and regular parents will not detect abnormal behaviors with only a cursory, un-mindful look especially as S/Os may appear to be doing what is normal behavior right in front of a parent.

S/Os may give side-hugs, as people working with children are now required to do, but allow their hand to drift downwards to the waist, or even lower, for a short time, or linger longer than normal in the hug. An arm around the shoulder may result in a short neck massage.

High-fiving can end with a prolonged hold instead of an instant release and even chosen over a quick fist-bump. An S/O might brush in front of an unsuspecting child. These subtle behaviors can be easily missed.

Dads wrestling on the floor with their kids is okay but when a 30-year-old uncle wrestles on the floor with his 12-year-old nephew and then sits beside him for the family meal rather than sitting with the adults, parents should take notice. Is this normal behavior? Would I do it? That uncle playing video games with his nephew, while all the other adults are clearing the tables and washing dishes, should ring a bell that calls for more attention. When a club leader or trainee invests excessive time in one or two children separate from the rest of the adult staff, parents (or other staff members) should take notice.

> The litmus test for recognizing concerning behavior being done to someone else is to ask ourselves the question "Would I do that?" If the answer is "No", then further investigation is warranted.

DISCLOSING INFORMATION

Information regarding CSA should obviously not be disclosed to a church at large. It is private information that should be shared by the family to perhaps the church pastor or a counsellor. Broadcasting the fact that a child has been sexually abused in the past may not only cause a S/O to think differently about a child and visualize what might have happened, but eroticize the child. As discussed

> **Broadcasting the information about former sexual abuse happenings attracts more sexual molestation.**

earlier, he knows that this child is less likely to tell on him should he sexually abuse him, or her. Broadcasting the information about former sexual abuse happenings attracts more sexual molestation, as blood in an ocean attracts sharks to their next meal.

RECOVERY AFTER SEXUAL ABUSE

Some children recover well after being sexually abused. For them it was just a bump in the road. This is especially so if adults believe them when they told them what happened and they obtain good support and counseling. A parent's over-reaction on hearing the report is likely to impede the child's recovery, but when parents are educated and informed about child abuse, their reaction should be more controlled, which will give their child a definite advantage in navigating the rest of their life.

A child is also likely to recover from sexual abuse more easily if the S/O was a neighbor down the street who then went to jail for a while, than if it was a family member. The neighbor may never come back to live in the same community. That child may even be praised for nailing the molester and believe that they did a good thing in reporting the abuse. However, if the abuser was a brother, step-father, father, uncle, aunt or some other family member, reporting that abuse will be more difficult and less likely to be believed even though only 2-12% of allegations made by children have been found to be untruthful. Reporting this abuse causes division in the family and when the S/O has done time in jail, they will be returned to that child's family forever. The child cannot escape living through repeated unhealthy situations so excellent counseling is extremely important. The fact is that about 98% of S/Os are released to the community in less than 10 years, depending on state regulations, which is a comparatively short time in a child's life.

Both child and parent should avail themselves of counseling and guidance provided through "the system" and private counseling if they can afford, or obtain it.

REDUCING THE RISK OF CSA

No single action will ensure that a child will not be abused sexually, however there are a number of actions a family, or church, can take to reduce the risk of this happening. Jensen (2016) listed many of the following points.

- Talk age-appropriately with your children about sexual matters. Those who grow up with parent-child discussions about sexual behaviors are more likely to report it when it does happen.

- Talk with your child from the age of three or four about safety matters repeatedly, not as a one-time talk. This should be 4-5 times a year and should not only be about CSA. It should be mixed in with wearing helmets when riding bikes, skateboards or snowboards, gun safety, bullying, wearing seatbelts, honesty, body piercing, swimming safety, how to answer the door, talking to strangers etc.

- "Good touch, bad touch, secret touch" should be discussed so that a child can intelligently detect something that is not right. Hugs should not be full on, lengthy or make a child feel uncomfortable. It is okay to refuse to participate in any hugging that is uncomfortable. Side hugging is a good practice however "good touch, bad touch" should not stand alone. It is confusing because it assumes that

S/Os are mean and hurtful in their action. This is usually not the case because they try to make touch feel good, even enjoyed, and may make into a game. They may give the child treats too. A child who does not receive love from a parent, may feel special and loved when receiving attention from an adult while not aware that this is the wrong kind of love. By adding "secret touch" to "good touch, bad touch" one gives an irrefutable indicator as to what is not okay. Children understand what a secret is, and telling them that that it is not okay to be asked to keep *this* secret, is important. It should be a bright red flag to parents/guardians. "Secret touch" is never to be tolerated despite bribes or threats.

• Private parts are private and should not be looked at or touched by others, nor should a child touch others'

> **No sexual approach is the child's fault even if it happened a while back.**

private parts. Parents today are raising the next generation of S/Os and taking this action *is* primary prevention of CSA. Private parts should not be viewed on electronic devices either –ever.

- No sexual approach is the child's fault even if it happened a while back and children need to know it is important to always tell a parent or trusted adult.

- Always use the correct anatomical term when referring to male and female body parts. Using a term like "kitty" or "purse" for the vagina can result in us overlooking, or at least causing a delay in understanding that a child is reporting inappropriate sexual acts.

- Predators may play the sympathy card to discourage a child from telling on them. Their behavior is not excusable due to illness or sickness. It is a calculated, carefully planned behavior.

- Parents need to pay attention and intervene (when appropriate) by reporting their concerns to a pastor or group leader, depending on where the situation occurred *and* if these are only *suspicions*. However, if the situation is real, and *not* just a suspicion, telling a mandatory reporter still does not get them off the hook if that mandatory reporter fails to make the report. Usually there is a 48-hour window to report the matter to the police or CPS, and the original reporter has an onus to confirm that this matter has indeed been reported. Anonymous reporting may be an option initially.

- Churches need to be involved and institute policies to protect children, investigate concerns, be watchful, determine the appropriateness of programs such as "Protect the Vulnerable", and sign up their congregations if they feel it appropriate.

- Churches should get discussions going about CSA and invite professionals who are versed in protecting children from sexual predators. They should provide workshops for their congregation and no longer be naïve. Child molesters *do* exist in our world, and churches need to be active and alert.

- New attendees should be checked out without paranoia but with informed concern remembering that less than 5% of a congregation are of any concern when considering child sexual abuse.

- Church administrators should provide education about CSA to pastoral staff and leaders about state laws regarding and reporting incidences promptly.

WHERE TO GO FROM HERE

Being attune to the realities of living in today's sinful world has resulted in resources being developed to help

> **Together we can make a difference –one child at a time.**

churches, parents, family members, teachers, pastors, youth leaders and regular caring people to play a responsible role in protecting children. Together we can make a difference –one child at a time.

CHAPTER 9

THE SIN PROBLEM

The destructive nature of sin can be traced from its origin until the present time through the scriptures. A cursory look at the world today tells believers that the end of time is not far into the future. Some scoff at that idea while others decide that it won't happen in their life-time because their parents and grandparents were saying the same thing a quarter or half a century ago –and it hasn't happened! Although Christian faiths differ over many biblical truths, most Christians are adventists – they believe that Jesus will return to Earth a second time as prophesied in the Bible. They also agree that the Bible sets the standard for living and how to treat one another. But not all Christians agree on who is their neighbor. Could the Bible possibly say that pedophiles, or worse –that child molesters are their neighbors, and that they should love them? Surely not. God wouldn't ask Christians to love *them*. Or perhaps He would.

Being a Christian, or a pedophile is not mutually exclusive. Pedophiles sit in church pews and worship God alongside other sinners. Everyone is tainted by sin "for all have sinned, and fall short of the glory of God (Romans 3:23)," and all are in need of a Savior. The two groups, Christians and pedophiles, are cordial, and even friendly towards one another, that is until the pedophile's story it exposed. VPs correctly believe that should their innermost psyche be exposed –even to a church community, they will be classed as monsters who should be kept far away from children and from those whose sanitized sins of pride, arrogance, lust, criticism, deceit, intolerance, hate, back-biting, demonizing pedophiles and more, can in no way be compared with the dirty, dark secrets of the pedophilic mind—even though they haven't acted on that attraction.

Christians (and society) have yet to understand that pedophiles are guilty of nothing for *being* pedophiles, nor are they guilty for their sexual *desire,* but they *are* accountable for their sexual behavior. In understanding this, Christians should treat pedophiles as Jesus treated lepers in His day, like sinners in need of healing and acceptance.

> Christians (and society) have yet to understand that pedophiles are guilty of nothing for *being* pedophiles, nor are they guilty for their sexual *desire*, but they are accountable for their sexual behavior.

Everyone struggles with sin, even the apostle Paul. In Romans 7:15 he wrote, "I do not understand what I do. For what I want to do I do not do, but what I hate I do." Does that sound familiar? People *plan* on never committing their pet sin again, only to find they have done it. Somehow it happened again. Why this happens is partially explained in Romans 7:18: "I know that nothing good lives in me, that is, in my sinful nature. For I have the desire to do what is good, but I cannot carry it out."

BIG AND LITTLE SINS

Society may wonder which sins are little sins, and which fall into the *big* sin category. The apostle Paul answers that quandary in Romans 6:23: "For the wages of sin is death; but the gift of God is eternal life through Jesus

Christ our Lord." Paul does not differentiate between *big* sins and *little* sins. According to the apostle, sin is sin. This means that the sanitized sins that Christians would hate to think of as *big* sins are equal in God's sight to the whoppers –and God yet doesn't care! He did not die on the cross for only big sins, but for any sin. End of sentence. Christians are just like everyone else because "There is no one righteous, not even one (Romans 3:10)." We are all on the same par – sinners, and yet God still loves us.

Few will dispute that someone who molests a child has committed a bad sin, one of the worst, but to God any sin is bad. If VPs act on their sexual attraction, they would commit a sin that is unacceptable to society but no one can say they didn't sin today. By even saying that, they would be lying –which would put an end to their so-called perfection. But every day God invites everyone to ask Him to forgive them for their sins and to give them strength to overcome their own sinful nature –their pet sin, their sanitized sin, in His power. So too can a VP ask the Lord to help them maintain their purity and enter into no sexual interaction with a child, nor fantasizing.

> A VP can ask the Lord to help them maintain their purity and enter into no sexual interaction with a child.

While on earth, Jesus decried the uselessness of ceremonies and external holiness. Jesus showed the people that healing on Sabbath was not breaking the Sabbath, and nor was God a God of vengeance, but a God of love for "God is love (1 John 4:8)." He showed the common people a new and better way of living, but the Jewish leaders were so wrapped up in what they had built their religion into being, that they missed the Messiah when He came to earth and crucified Him as a common criminal. Jesus' way *was* different, so much so that after His ascension, His disciples were accused of turning the world "upside down" (Acts 17:6 NKJV).

GOD WORKING IN US

In taking this new view of pedophilia, Christ's followers today might be accused of turning the world upside down, of being naïve or soft in the head. By beginning to provide a listening ear and an open mind to VPs who are battling with their sinful nature, Christians (and anyone who truly understands a pedophile's struggles) can follow Jesus' example of reaching Untouchables. Christ's forgiveness and grace gives VPs a hope of victory, even as they battle with a life-long attraction.

Some VPs may experience an instant makeover when they accept the recreating power of the Holy Spirit in their lives, but for most it will be a daily journey. Sometimes it will be an almost overwhelming battle to remain pure, but victory can be gained when sinners are connected to the transforming power of Jesus. First Corinthians 10:13 says: "No temptation has seized you except what is common to man. And God is faithful; He will not let you to be tempted beyond what you can bear. But when you are tempted, He will also provide a way out so that you can stand up under it." That promise puts God's reputation on the line. But we can choose to trust the Bible for God is truth (John 14:6) and He does not lie (Titus 1:2).

That message should bring hope to pedophiles who trust God's promises and to anyone who struggles with sin of any ilk. That means everybody. Satan seeks to control every single person in an attempt to ultimately win the Great Controversy, the battle between good and evil, between God and himself. He works especially hard to win the allegiance of those who are striving to leave their sinful lives behind them.

The promise in 1 Corinthians 10:13 does not mean

that people will never be tempted to be prideful, arrogant, critical, lustful, intolerant, deceitful and back-biting ever again, nor can MAPs assume that they will be free of their sexual orientation and the risk of acting on it. Everyone, without exception, is tempted to perform their pet sin (or attraction) –but the temptation will *not* be greater than they can bear. With Jesus Christ's power within them, *all* sinners can be victorious over their inherent tendencies that could lead to dangerous thoughts, or may lead to active sinning, no matter what sin may be their downfall.

At creation man was given the power of choice. This made him superior to other living creatures and it is with this gift of choice that people can decide to walk daily with the Lord, or not. Just as the alcoholic or drug addict can choose repeatedly to be victorious for another minute, day, week or year by relying on

> God keeps on loving each individual despite Him knowing them better than they know themselves! That is His amazing grace!

the Lord, so too can the sinner live as a recovering sinner –but still a sinner. They cannot claim to have reached the stage of no longer *being* an addict or a sinner –or a pedophile, but in the power of the Holy Spirit they can live life to the fullest in Christ, without acting on their desire, just as can anyone else who trusts in the power and grace of God. What is incredible is that God keeps on loving each individual despite Him knowing them better than they know themselves! That is His amazing grace!

Intellectually believers know that sin is no surprise to an Omniscient God for after all He is all-knowing, but confessing their sins to Him can be challenging despite knowing that the act of confessing sins to the Lord draws the heart of the sinner into a stronger relationship with Him. It opens them up to the continued working of the Holy Spirit in their lives. As evangelist Mike Tucker clearly put it, "God's grace is bigger than your sin (Tucker, 2016)," Any sin. Later Tucker listed some of the sinners saved by grace that he expected to see in the heavenly kingdom like drug abusers, pedophiles and members of ISIS. That is something to think about!

A LOST RELATIONSHIP RESTORED

After the very first sin, Adam and Eve immediately felt shame and made fig-leaf clothing in an attempt to hide their nakedness from God. They then *hid* themselves from Him. Obviously they intellectually limited God's all-knowingness if they thought He did not know where they were! When He found them, (as if they were lost), Adam blamed Eve for his sin and Eve blamed the serpent –that God had incidentally created, for her sin (Genesis 3:11-13). How quickly their sins multiplied, and they still do today. But it took just one sin, one bad choice, to forever break the beautiful relationship between God and man.

However God, the loving God so many worship today, didn't leave Adam and Eve to die without hope. He revealed to them the promise of a Redeemer and the hope of a perfectly restored existence.

FORGIVENESS

The Bible contains good news. 1 John 1:9 says, "If we confess our sins, he is faithful and just to forgive us our sins, and to purify us from all unrighteousness." Centuries before we read King David's words in Psalm 32:2-5. He eloquently described the pain he felt when he failed to acknowledge his sin before God and the peace that came when he confessed his sin to God "and you (God) forgave the guilt of my sin."

Most adults can recall a time in childhood when they lied to their parents or stole from them, cheated in school or got a friend into trouble. They remember the fear, shame and uncomfortableness that came with it. But when they finally plucked up courage and confessed their sin to the person they had slighted, a weight rolled off their shoulders and life became good again.

Committing sins against another person as an adult may be more complex than any childhood indiscretion, and confession does not automatically result in people offering forgiveness to the confessor. However, the act of truly confessing a sin releases us from the weight of guilt and brings a beauty and peace that unconfessed sin cannot equal. Joy and freedom come alive when we confess our sins to God and are relieved of the burden it places on our mind and heart. Jesus invites us to share our burdens with Him, not just our sins, and find true rest in Him (Matthew 11:28) and then, like Jesus said to the woman caught in adultery, we should "go and sin no more (John 8:11)."

One important point to remember is that human forgiveness can only be given by a victim. No one is in a position to offer forgiveness to another for an action that was taken against someone else.

True repentance and confession of sins is one important step towards rebuilding a relationship with God. Just like the Father in the story of the prodigal son (Luke 15:1-24) was waiting for his son to return from a far land where he had wasted his money on sinful living, so God is watching and waiting for each sinner to return to the Creator God. God does not forget His children but He allows them to exert their free will, which may result in them drifting into sinful ways and separating themselves from Him. He *always* wants to renew that personal relationship between Himself and His child.

Jesus' disciples had been exposed to prayer but needed to know what *real* prayer should be. They asked Him to teach them how to pray. The Lord's Prayer (Luke 11:2-4) was His answer which begins by addressing God directly as "Father" or "Daddy". God requires no intermediary human being to speak to Him on the sinner's behalf. As His sons and daughters, we have direct access to Him. He is always ready to hear the simplest, sincere prayer of any of His children. He is never too busy to hear their prayers of adoration, thankfulness, requests that are in harmony with His will and confessions. He is their ever loving heavenly Father.

GOD'S LOVE FOR MANKIND

Peter beautifully describes the Father's love for His children, the human family. "The Lord is not slow in keeping his promise, as some understand slowness. He is patient with you, not wanting anyone to perish, but everyone to come to repentance (2 Peter 3:9). During the three years Peter was discipled by Jesus, he saw the Father's character displayed by the Son. John records Jesus saying to Philip, "Anyone who has seen me, has seen the Father. How can you say 'Show us the Father?' (John 14:9)." That is very plain

James, Jesus' brother, instructs his readers in a new level of confession. "Confess your faults one to another, and pray one for another, that ye may be healed. The effectual fervent prayer of a righteous man availeth much (James 5:16. KJV)." Is James asking sinners to stand up in front of their church and unburden themselves of their guilt by recounting their sins in graphic detail to enthralled listeners? This does not appear to be a healthy option. Most likely James is not telling them to broadcast their sins, their sexual fantasies, their most recent acts of pompous pride or gluttony or raging anger, but their *faults*, which are their *propensities* or *inexplicable desire* to sin. Sinful behaviors are to be confessed to God but their yet-to-be acted upon propensity to sin with which they struggle, is to be confessed to "one another", in confidence. Unfortunately some "Christians" won't listen.

Many Christians believe that everyone is born with a sinful nature and therefore everyone has a propensity to evil. Over the last 6000 years Satan has studied the human family and knows how to trick people into sinning more. His main focus is not on those already caught in his snares and practicing evil, but on those who are trying to withstand evil and maintain a relationship with God. So the faults James advises them to confess to one another (not a church-full), are the character traits and deficits that drag them down time and again despite their best effort to remain constantly connected to God. Without the power of Christ in them, sinners are no a match for the wily Devil. Their *propensity* for pride, arrogance, selfishness, anger, lust or any sexual sin like adultery, fornication, pornography and other sexual improprieties, hatefulness, impatience, indolence, intolerance, greed, pedophilia and other unlovely traits of character, are an on-going battle. By neglecting to wage war in Christ's power against these faults, these propensities, will take deeper root and become sinful behaviors.

> **Without the power of Christ in them, sinners are no a match for the wily Devil.**

WORKING IN PARTNERSHIP WITH GOD

With an understanding of pedophilia the Christian can learn how to better treat MAPs and most importantly, work wisely towards preventing child sexual abuse. Some Christians may even come to the place where they are willing to listen compassionately to a pedophile reveal (confess) his most-scary, inner fault –that he is a MAP, a VP, someone loathed by society and assumed to be unable to change, a virtual ticking time-bomb.

> The Christian can learn how to better treat MAPs and most importantly, work wisely towards preventing child sexual abuse.

But the mind-blowing truth is that Jesus *can* and *does* change people's lives if they truly desire such a make-over. He *is* the Life Changer. It may be a hard-fought battle but when the desires of the heart are changed through the power of Jesus Christ at the deepest level, then the behavior changes. MAPs will still live with their sexual orientation, but the healing touch of Jesus can lessen their desire to act on their sexual attraction, enable them to control it and possibly even remove it completely. In John 16:3,24 Jesus invites us to ask for "anything" in His name that is according to His will and He promises we will receive it. Surely, this would include freedom from the powers of the Deceiver? Believe that God can bring about change that extends to *any* seemingly intractable sin.

Some mature Christians will feel honoured to have this deep, private, dark secret fault confessed to them. Perhaps some are ready to put an arm around the confessor and say, "Thank-you for trusting me with your struggle." By exposing a secret, it loses much of its potency in that single act (Quinn, 2015 p.59). Christ's follower may be able to offer a prayer for the MAP right then, and with compassion and sincerity ask God to continue giving them victory over their sinful nature. That brother or sister in Christ can claim the promise that the prayers of a faithful Christian will support them as they continue on a victorious path. Prayer is powerful.

Christiansen (2016) describes the uncomfortable reality of today. "There is a god in this world who is a monster, and that is Satan. He is responsible for all suffering, all disease, all disasters, all unhappiness. And he will do anything he can to place the blame for all this on God." Satan has a stranglehold on this planet and yet he will not get traction if Christians boldly live as light (Matthew 5:14,16) and salt (Matthew 5:13) in their communities.

In the Sermon on the Mount Jesus called His followers to be these two elements, light and salt, and has placed Christians exactly where He needs them to be to reduce CSA through their daily intercessory prayers for that brother or sister. The harvest of souls brought to Christ through

> Satan has a stranglehold on this planet and yet he will not get traction if Christians boldly live as light and salt in their communities.

their prayers may not be known in their life time but will be revealed in the kingdom. As the Christian community responds with understanding and compassion to such confessions and works in partnership with the Holy Spirit to change the world one MAP at a time, kids will be saved from CSA.

The Christian community will recognize the amazing courage of a sinner who confesses the most intimate depths of their soul to a fellow traveller who prays for God to uplift them and give them victory over their struggle. His name will be praised.

Even Jesus needed someone to help Him carry His cross out of Jerusalem to Golgotha (Matthew 27:32). Simon of Cyrene was that helper. Christians can be a

Simon of Cyrene to the sincere MAP and help him carry his cross of pedophilia. They can be accountability partners, prayer partners, their confidante, sponsor or mentor. Fellow travellers along life's journey do not know when they will need a Simon to help them through a personal struggle.

In response to actively ministering to the needs of a MAP, Christians might themselves develop the courage to reveal their innermost faults to another Christ-filled person who can partner with them by praying to God for their victory. They may develop the courage to remove the mask they wear to church every week. Wearing it has made them feel secure and without it they are fearful of what others will think of them when their duplicitous holiness is revealed. Maybe they are embarrassed to be struggling with faults that betray weaknesses and apparent worthlessness. Perhaps they believe that confessing their faults to people who used to place them on a pedestal of assumed spiritual purity, will destroy them. But they too can feel the sweet peace of forgiveness and power to live a life committed to God.

Paul gives Christ's followers an important role to play in caring for the spiritual needs of others. "If someone is caught in a sin, you who are spiritual should restore him gently. But watch yourself, or you also may be tempted (Galatians 6:1-3)." Everyone is spiritually wounded, perhaps more so than they realize, but as they minister to one another, healing can come to both parties. When someone sins, it is no time to gloat over their predicament for they may be next! But, by restoring a struggling believer to a renewed faith in the Lord, God's grace is multiplied. What a blessing it is to them both to be a part in the destabilization of the Devil. He will lose his footing against a multitude of prayer warriors who uphold each other in Christ.

It is time for Christians to join hands and do battle with the Devil who is like a roaring lion looking for his quarry. He knows his time is short (1 Peter 5:8; Revelation 12:12). The good news is that 2000 years ago Christ won that war against the Devil on the cross, and now in partnership with Him, His followers can help others win their battle with sin.

CHAPTER 10

TOUCHING UNTOUCHABLES

Pastor Walt walked up to the podium. Would his church members be upset to hear his message from God about a very sensitive matter? Was it a message from God, or actually a message from George or both? Of one thing, he was sure, actively preventing CSA was very important, and in learning about pedophilia, his church would strengthen their power to protect children.

He knew his little congregation well, from the elderly couple who sat on the right-front, to Bethany, the outspoken church member who often rubbed others up (and down) the wrong way. He was certain he would hear from her right after the sermon.

"Good morning Friends. Today, let us open the Scriptures at 2 Corinthians 3:18."

Pastor Walt paused and then began reading, "But we all, with unveiled face, beholding as in a mirror the glory of the Lord, are being transformed into the same image from glory to glory, just as by the Spirit of God."

"For a while I have been troubled by how faith based communities treat people who do not look like them, eat the same foods as they do, wear the same clothes or act like them. What are Christ's followers doing to show these people God's love? *Are we* showing them His love? So today we're going to explore that some more."

"Last week when I was out running, I listened to three interesting podcasts from Family Life Today (2016) which piqued my interest on how the power of Christ can change anyone who is open to the working of the Holy Spirit in their lives. Two pastors were interviewed. They had recently published a book titled, "Transforming Homosexuality. What the Bible says about sexual orientation and change (2015)." Although homosexuality is not the sexual orientation I am focusing on today, they talked about the transforming power of God in *anyone* with a sin problem, including homosexuals, and their ideas tied in well with today's sermon. So let's take a look at how God can work in our lives."

"We know we can't look into another person's heart like the Lord can, and we can't see the burdens they are carrying, even if they look just like us and are socializing in the same circle and worshiping with us. But, I ask you, how do we relate to others whose sexual orientation we do not understand? Bisexuals, transgenders, gays…and now I have to admit my concern for the pedophilic population."

"A month ago we touched on that topic, and, before you throw rotten tomatoes at me –or get up and leave, I am asking you to give me a chance to explain. Yes, I have George to thank for some of these thoughts, but surely we, as people who say we follow Jesus' example, owe it to pedophiles to hear them out and see if we can understand their situation better?"

"I think we have all heard George talk about virtuous pedophiles and understand that these people have a sexual attraction towards children but do not act on it. Let me make it clear, I am not talking about child molesters although, in understanding pedophilia better we might grasp some of the struggles this group has too."

"The Bible consistently speaks lovingly of children. The first command given by God to Adam in Eve was for them to be 'fruitful and increase in number (Genesis 1:28),' –to have children. One of the distinctive marks of the chosen people, the Israelites, was that they did not to follow the customs of the surrounding nations who worshiped gods other than the true God, Jehovah. One such false god was Molech, a god of the Ammonites, into whose gaping fiery mouth worshipers threw their own children to appease Molech. God warmed them not to follow these practices. He was clear: 'Let no one be found among you who sacrifices his son or daughter in the fire… Anyone who does this thing is detestable to the Lord (Deuteronomy 18:10-12).' The warning was not heeded and almost a 1000 years later God's prophet Jeremiah told wayward Israel that was building 'high places of Baal to burn their sons in the fire as offerings to Baal –something I (God) do not command…nor did it enter my mind (Jeremiah 19:8),' to stop this terrible practice. God did not change but Israel did not heed the warnings. In evil King Ahaz' reign 'he sacrificed his sons in the fire, following the detestable ways of the nations' surrounding Judah (2 Chronicles 28:3), which contributed to his early downfall. Then, in Micah's time the people got the same message: Don't sacrifice your children for your sins but 'act justly and love mercy and walk humbly with your God (Micah 6:7, 8).' Children were to be loved, protected and cared for then –and now."

"In Psalms 127:3, 5 (NKJV) we read that 'Children are a heritage of the Lord…Happy is the man that hath his quiver full of them.' Children are a blessing from the Lord even if we as parents know that they have their moments when we might consider them otherwise!"

"In the New Testament we find that Jesus was no different during his ministry on earth. In Matthew 18:2 Jesus' disciples were vying for leadership positions in what they thought would be a victorious government led by Jesus. He used a child to show them what was truly important –to be humble and eager to learn. He went on and said, 'And whoever welcomes a little child like this in my name, welcomes me (Matthew 18:5).' We get the picture, Jesus cared about children. A little later there is the story about mothers bringing their children to Jesus for a blessing. This story is recorded in all but John's gospel

(Matthew 19:13-15; Mark 10:13-16; Luke 18:15-17). It held an important message. The disciples shooed the children away saying that Jesus was much too busy to bother with little children but Jesus didn't agree. He rebuked His disciples and said, 'Let the little children come to me … for the kingdom of heaven belongs to such as these (Matthew 19:14).'"

"You're probably familiar with many other instances in the Bible that show God loves children and you probably know two favorite children's songs: 'Jesus loves me this I know' and 'Jesus loves the little children, all the children of the world.' These songs clearly give the message that Jesus, and by extension God, loves children, and so should we as His followers."

"John recorded Jesus using the term, 'little children (John 13:33)' in addressing His disciples immediately before He was taken captive in the Garden at Gethsemane. Jesus was acting like a loving father trying to protect his children from what He knew was about to happen. The apostle Paul, although he apparently had no children of his own, uses 'my little children' as a form of endearment in writing letters to the churches he had started (Galatians 4:19 NKJV) and John used 'my little children' multiple times as a salutation of kindness (1 John 2:1, 12, 13, 1 John 4:4 NKJV). When closing his first epistle he wrote, 'Little children, keep yourselves from idols. Amen (1 John 5:21 NKJV).' These words may read 'dear children' in your Bible translation and show John's tender-heartedness as a teacher. No doubt John learned this salutation by being around Jesus."

"Another slant on this topic of loving children is that James, Jesus' brother, tells the new Christians to care for children's needs. They were vulnerable. James says, 'Religion that God our Father accepts as pure and faultless is this: to look after orphans and widows in their distress (James 1:27),' and Paul admonishes 'fathers do not exasperate your children (Ephesians 6:4)' or 'provoke them to anger'. From these texts it is clear that Jesus' followers recognized children as precious souls who needed protection and care. We should still be doing this."

"Today most cultures recognize physical, emotional, verbal and sexual abuse of children as unacceptable. Molesting a child should never be mistaken for love and sexual intimacy. God instituted marriage for sexual intimacy to be

> **Molesting a child should never be mistaken for love and sexual intimacy.**

between a man and woman within the marriage covenant. This special love was a gift from God. The Old and New Testaments contain many texts that express God's dislike of sexual perversion (1 Corinthian 6:18, Galatians 5:19-21), but our world ignores the Biblical instruction and has become confused and down-right rebellious. Often Christians choose to ignore the fact that God invented sex to be a beautiful relationship within marriage. I haven't preached about the beauty of sexual intimacy as God ordained it for a while, nor have I preached about the perversions of sexual behavior that are so prominent in today's society. The Bible is very clear as to what is right or wrong but is it any wonder that our young people –and young people in general, are confused about homosexuality, transgender issues and sexual identity which are common locker-room talk in junior high? By failing to discuss these topics, we allow Satan's perversions to gain traction in our kids' minds before their brains are fully developed. So today, I am taking up George's topic regarding people who are sexually attracted to children and trying to build on what is clear in the Bible and what should be our role as light and salt in the earth."

"First though, let me make it clear, never ever can

sexually assaulting a child be justified. It is always wrong. Let's remember that there's a war going on between good and evil, God and Satan. We know that Satan, the father of lies, will twist anything God says and make it appear the reverse. He muddies the boundaries so skilfully that it can be hard to know just when a boundary is actually crossed until we find ourselves far into treacherous waters."

"With respect to pedophilia we should no longer automatically assume that when someone admits to having a sexual attraction to children that he is acting on that attraction. We now know better. We should look behind such a desperate admission to see someone who needs understanding because he may be almost at the point of suicide. He is a person who needs to know that he is loved by God and that we want to understand."

A pedophile may feel he has a big 'P' painted on their forehead which can never be removed just as the letter A, for adultery, was plastered on Hester Pryne's breast in Nathaniel Hawthorne's classic, The Scarlet Letter. That isn't so. Everyone is so much more than their sexual orientation, as are minor attracted people. They are fathers, sisters, cousins, brothers, teachers, professionals, baristas, neighbours, colleagues, friends and more, who are, incidentally, sexually attracted to certain children even though they choose not to act on it. Just like others may be sexually attracted to somebody else's wife, or husband, or a work colleague, while married to their own spouse. Hopefully they choose not to act on that attraction. Unfortunately suicide is a permanent solution to a mistreated problem for virtuous pedophiles in their lonely, untouchable condition. We can help them avoid taking this step. We can assist them in finding professional help. We can support them as they come out to friends and family and journey on through life. We can be part of the solution, not their problem."

"Friends, Satan takes every opportunity he can to lead people away from God's perfect way and towards the dark side. Time is getting short. He is pulling out all the stops. It is not a matter of business as usual and child abuse is fair game for Satan. He knows the scriptures better than any Christian or biblical scholar, and He knows that Jesus is returning soon. He knows Revelation 1:7 which says, 'Look, he is coming with the clouds, and every eye will see him.' Satan is aware that

> **Satan knows the scriptures better than any Christian or biblical scholar, and He knows that Jesus is returning soon.**

prophecies pointing to the second coming of Christ have almost all been fulfilled and that earth's history is nearing its close. He can see the second hand of the clock is moving towards midnight and he is desperate to bring as much pain, evil and deception as possible. He is unscrupulous and knows what the end of time means for him. Curtains. His final, eternal destruction."

"Thankfully the Bible is filled with promises that give hope to us all if confess our sins and in the power of Jesus 'go and sin no more'. No one is excluded. No matter what may have be our pet sin, we, like pedophiles, need not despair. The Bible encourages us to take the next step and come of the foot of the cross where we can find forgiveness."

"So let's go back and remind ourselves of the text we started with in 1 Corinthians 3:18: 'But we all, with unveiled face, beholding as in a mirror the glory of the Lord, are being transformed into the same image from glory to glory, just as by the Spirit of God.'"

"This is a transformational verse that holds so much promise, so much hope for every one of us. The people in Corinth were not exactly shining examples of the Christian church. They had a lot of problems, including sexual immorality, but Paul focused on encouraging the struggling believers in Corinth and us today. All of us are being transformed by the power of the Holy Spirit as we look to Jesus and invite the Holy Spirit to work in our lives, to convict us of our wrongs. It is not a maybe, or perhaps. We *are being transformed* into His image when we behold Jesus. This verse doesn't mean we will be sinless but it has the key to making this transformation happen –beholding Jesus. Friends, this can happen no matter what our sin problem is and it can also give hope to non-offending, and even offending minor attracted people. The Holy Spirit can transform their lives as they behold Jesus and allow the Holy Spirit to transform their lives. What an amazing promise! And it is ours for the taking. We just need to keep our eyes on Jesus."

"The Bible is replete with hope for everyone, all sinners, not just sexual sinners but before we read a selection of these promises, I want to clearly tell you that I am not asking you to take any teen, or parent or single person that may have a hint of sexual attraction to children and think you are up to praying pedophilia away. It is not that simple. But…with a newfound understanding of the *possible* journey ahead of this person, and an intelligent, loving, un-shockable mind that has *some* insight into what might be behind their comment or question, you can assist them in finding professional help, on-line support or even be that Christian to talk with them and help them on their journey of healing."

"I am not so naïve to tell you that there are no dangerous pedophiles studying children's behavior and activities or, as some call it 'grooming' children. Probably they're grooming those least likely to tell on them, or least likely to be believed, or even grooming a vulnerable parent so that they can gain access to their children. These dangerous people might be leaders of our church, our youth fellowship or on our pastoral staff, but let us remember that God is still in the business of reclaiming *all* sinners, of transforming every life –but these ones are probably outside your league."

"Others, especially those in their teen years, can be enticed by Satan into a downward spiral by innocently watching anime or manga cartoons on line which may lead into offensive pornographic cartoons. Looking at sexualized cartoons can become a habit and lead to more serious child pornography. We need to be knowingly on the alert to the problem and not become hysterical at the slightest hint of this behavior, or run and bury our head in the sand."

"Let's remember that God cares about children, that He loves them (Matthew 18:5) and hates injustice, and hates for evil to come to any child (Psalm 72: 2, 4, 2-14). With this in mind, let's read two of many promises in the Bible."

"**John 8:11**. '"Neither do I condemn you," Jesus declared. "Go now and leave your life of sin."'

- Jesus said this to a woman who was caught in the act adultery. How she came to be accused is not clear from the Scriptures but Jesus did not side with her accusers but gave her hope. He gives each of us hope today even in cases of sexual sin."

"**1 John 1:9** 'If we confess our sins, he is faithful and just and will forgive us our sins and purify us from all unrighteousness.'

- John has no doubt that Jesus Christ was and is a Man of His word. If we confess our sins with sincerity He *will* forgive us and cleanse us from our past wrong actions. That is God's amazing grace."

"Let me remind you that God is gracious and merciful and available to help us in our struggles with sexual sins, with pot or tobacco or drugs, with greed, lust, pride, alcohol, anger, hate, impatience and other sanitized sins —whatever our challenge is. He knows your propensities and wants to help you be victorious. He is a prayer away and *will* answer your request for victory over temptation."

"For the minor-attracted person who depends on Jesus Christ to maintain their virtuous status, they can be assured of help too and can claim victory in the power of the Lord."

"As your Pastor, I want to encourage you to recognize not only your innermost needs but the needs of others who you may not understand. God *does* understand them and will work in their lives too. Absolutely no sin is beyond His forgiveness. Our part is to recognize *our* sinful propensities —and at times our actions, and turn from them, asking for His forgiveness. We can leave the sins of others up to the Holy Spirit whose job it is to convict them. It's not our job."

"We must remember that minor-attracted persons, pedophiles, are not committing a sin by being pedophiles.

> **Minor-attracted persons, pedophiles, are not committing a sin by being pedophiles.**

It is only if they act on their attraction that a sin is committed so we should not treat them as sinners beyond the reach of God. Perhaps they were abused as children, perhaps their parents or grandparents were a poor genetic gene pool, perhaps they chose to associate with the wrong group of people –but whatever the case, they may feel they have nowhere to turn to for help now. But, should they acknowledge their vulnerability and need before God or to a trusted believer, we should listen empathetically and try to understand where they are coming from –not condemn them outright or become hysterical."

"So Friends, what is the church's role? Why are we here?"

"I want to read to you a few lines from Philip Yancey's book 'CHURCH: why bother?' That is a question we should be asking ourselves. Here is his answer. 'Having experienced the grace of God for ourselves, we wanted to dispense it to others, free of charge, no strings attached, as grace always comes. The church, I have learned, can indeed be a new sign radically dissimilar to the world's own manner, and contradict it in a way which is full of promise. For this reason, church is worth the bother.'"

"Christ's followers, His church, are called to protect the vulnerable – the children, and should reach out and touch today's Untouchables just as Jesus touched the untouchables of His day, two thousand years ago."

"Jesus told His followers to love their enemies (Matthew 5:44; Luke 6:27, 35). That is a huge challenge but in His power we can learn to love our enemies and those we do not understand. We can help minor-attracted persons in their search for professional assistance *before* they act on their attraction, be understanding of their struggle and maybe even become a compassionate accountability partner. Some of us could journey with them as they find healing from past wounds. We are all blighted by sin. We all have wounds that need healing and the bottom line is that we, the Church, should be salt and light in our communities. God can use us to reach the hurting— and Untouchables."

"Child molestation is still a sad reality in a planet embattled in a serious war between good and evil. Christ's death on Calvary assured us of victory in Christ Jesus but for now we must protect children and the vulnerable. Jesus Christ can 'do immeasurably more than all we ask or imagine, according to His power that is at work within us (Ephesians 3:20).' The 'more than we can imagine' includes healing and forgiveness. We can partner with Him in protecting children and in bringing restoration to minor attracted people before they act on their attraction."

"Reaching out to the minor-attracted person may not be your skill-set yet –or ever be, but there is much for us to learn with this particular group of people and no doubt George has many answers to help us. We can all be loving, accepting and gracious to those who want to be touched by the Savior's healing hand. We can no longer turn our backs on people for whom Jesus died and treat them as worthless."

"We, as Christ's followers, are called to be salt and light in this world, and yet each one of us is a sinner. As such we

> We can no longer turn our backs on people for whom Jesus died and treat them as worthless.

must allow for God to do a make-over within us, so that we can be God's hands in human form. We will then be able to get down beside the distressed, the marginalized, the unloved and unlovely, the despondent and hopeless –

and minor attracted people, and make our church a place where *all* sinners will come and feel His healing touch."

"In closing, I ask you to come to the cross of Christ and make room for one more next to you. Let's sing 'Room at the Cross for You.'"

ROOM AT THE CROSS FOR YOU

The cross upon which Jesus died,
Is a shelter in which we can hide;
And its grace so free is sufficient for me,
And deep is its fountain as wide as the sea.
   Chorus:
   There's room at the cross for you,
   There's room at the cross for you,
   Tho' millions have come,
   There's still room for one,
   Yes, there's room at the cross for you.

Tho' millions have found Him a friend,
And have turned from the sins they have sinned,
The Savior still waits to open the gates
And welcome a sinner before it's too late.
Chorus

The hand of my Savior is strong,
And the love of my Savior is long;
Through sunshine or rain, through loss and in gain,
The blood flows from Calvary to cleanse every stain.
Chorus

Pastor Walt paused. "Let us pray. Thank-you Lord God that Your love exceeds anything we can comprehend. Teach us how to love one another as You love us. In His blessed name we pray, Amen"

The postlude began quietly as Pastor Walt walked the few steps to the church door. His wife joined him at his side. How had his little congregation received his message?

Bethany took her place in line.

"A great sermon Pastor Walt. I guess I should first ask God for a make-over –and then I'll talk to George about his favorite ministry."

"Praise the Lord," Pastor Walt said and then turned to his wife.

"I think my message fell on listening ears. The Holy Spirit is at work. Praise God."

GLOSSARY OF TERMS

AOA	Age of attraction
ASAP	Website: ASAPinternational.org, the Association for Sexual Abuse Prevention
Aspies	People with Asperger syndrome
B4U-ACT	Website: b4uact.org
CPS	Child Protective Services
CSA	Child Sexual Abuse
DSM-5	American Psychiatric Association Diagnostic and Statistical Manual, 5th Edition
juvie	Juvenile detention center
KJV	Bible translation: King James Version
MAP	minor-attracted person; a person sexually attracted to children; virtuous pedophile
MHP	mental health professional
NKJV	Bible Translation: New King James Version
SAA	Sex Addicts Anonymous
S/O	Sex offender
VirPed	Website: virped.org
VP	virtuous pedophile, a pedophile who has not acted on their attraction; MAP

BIBLE TEXTS GIVING SINNERS HOPE

Jude 1:24,25. "To him who is able to keep you from falling, and to present you before his glorious presence without fault and with great joy... Amen".

- Can you hear the promise? Not only can God keep us from acting on our pet sins or sexual orientation or whatever, but He can present us to God as sin-free because He took our sins on Him when He died for us on the cross 2000 years ago. Let us accept His sacrifice for our sins, put our trust in Him and leave that sin-filled life behind.

Hebrews 12:2,3. "Let us fix our eyes on Jesus, the Author and Perfector of our faith, who for the joy set before him endured the cross, scorning its shame, and sat down at the right hand of the throne of God. Consider him who endured such opposition from sinful men, so that you will not grow weary and lose heart."

- We are all faced with big or small temptations and as we struggle through these distressing problems we can be encouraged to hold strong to the right if we could contemplate the magnitude of Jesus' gift for us and the humiliation and pain He endured for us. By doing, this we will be strengthened in our resolve to overcome our problems in His strength.

Romans 5:8. "But God demonstrates his own love for us in this: While we were still sinners, Christ died for us."

- God knows all about sin, our sins, and yet Jesus, God's Son, paid the ultimate price for our ugly sins by dying for us and giving us victory over sin through Him.

1 Peter 5:7. "Cast all your anxiety on him because He cares for you."

- What an invitation! Who is anxious or weighed down by cares? All of us, and yet God invites us to share our difficulties with Him. You can trust Him.

Titus 2:12-14 "It (the grace of God) teaches us to say no to ungodliness and worldly passions, and to live self-controlled, upright and godly lives in this present age, while we wait for the blessed hope –the glorious appearing of our great God and Saviour, Jesus Christ; who gave himself for us to redeem us from all wickedness."

- Jesus Christ is on our side. Attraction is not equal to action and in His power we can say "No" to Satan's sophistries and be victorious over *any* sinful propensity. We are all children of God. We have been bought with a price.

1 John 2:1,2 "My dear children, I write this to you so that you will not sin. But if anybody does sin, we have one who speaks to the Father in our defence –Jesus Christ the Righteous One."

- Jesus Christ will speak in our favor at judgement time. That does not mean that keeping on sinning is okay. We need to take the message in context. By confessing our sins (whatever they are) and accepting the changing power of the Holy Spirit in our lives, we live the best we can in accordance with God's will and *will* have Jesus Christ as our Advocate on the day of judgement. What could be better?

Hebrews 4:15. "For we do not have a high priest who is unable to sympathize with our weaknesses, but we have One who has been tempted in every way, just as we are – yet was without sin."

- Jesus was a sinless and saw sin close up. He knows what it is to be tempted for He was tempted in all things. He understand and the mercy we receive from the Lord, we can extend to others."

Philippians 1:6 "Being confident of this, that he who began a good work in you will carry it on to completion until the day of Christ Jesus."

- What a great encouragement! When we invite the Lord to work in us on our sinful behaviors, or tendencies, He is faithful. It doesn't matter what our short-fall was or is, He can transform our lives. He doesn't barge in and take over though, He will only come into our lives and do a make-over if we invite Him in. He won't give up on us either. He's in for the long haul. He paid a huge price for us by dying for our sins as a common criminal 2000 years ago. How amazing is that?

REFERENCES

- Abel, Gene. & Harlow, Nora. (2001) *The Stop child molestation book. What ordinary people can do in their everyday lives to save three million children.* Xlibris Corporation.

- Ackerman, A., Harris, A., Levenson, J., & Zgoba, K. (2011). *Who are the people in your neighborhood? A descriptive analysis of individuals on public S/O registries.* International Journal of Law and Psychiatry 34 (2011) 149–159. Retrieved on May 3, 2012 from http://files.mail-list.com/m/atsa/0-Ackerman-et-al-2012-JofCJ-RSO-rates.pdf.

- American Psychiatric Association. (2013) *Diagnostic and statistical manual of mental disorders. 5th Edition.* American Psychiatric Association, Washington DC.

- Beier, K. M. (2013) *BEDIT- The Berlin Dissexuality Therapy Program.* p.11

- Broomhall, Luke. (2016) *How do we protect our children from the unspeakable?* TEDxAdelaide, https://youtu.be/ZJaanSlb08A. April 1, 2016.

- Burk, Denny & Lambert, Heath. (2015) *Transforming homosexuality. What the Bible says about sexual orientation and change.* P&R Publishing Company, Phillipsburg, NJ.

- Cantor, James & McPhail, Ian. (2016) *Non-offending pedophiles.* p. 25, 26. (Pre-publication draft) April 2016.

- Christiansen, Scott. (2016) *The Zika virus, looking for answers.* Adventist World, p. 30-37. April 2016.

- Clark-Forey, Tracy. (2016) *'Virtuous pedophiles' put therapists in an ethical catch-22.* http://www.vocativ.com/315929/pedophiles-seeking-help-put-therapists-in-ethical-catch-22/ May 23, 2016.

- Cloud, John. (2003) *Pedophilia.* Time Magazine. http://content.time.com/time/magazine/article/0,9171,232584-1,00.html#ixzz0zwe10FiH. January 13, 2003.

- Dunkelfeld Project. (2015) *The German Dunkelfeld Project: A Pilot Study to Prevent Child Sexual Abuse and the Use of Child Abusive Images. Journal of Sexual Medicine,* Vol 12: 2. p. 529-542. February 2015. http://onlinelibrary.wiley.com/doi/10.1111/jsm.12785/abstract

- FamilyLife Today. (2016) Podcasts: Interviews with Denny Burk & Heath Lambert. May 17-19, 2016.

- Goode, D. Sarah. (2010) *Understanding and addressing adult sexual attraction to children. A study of paedophiles in contemporary society.* Routledge, New York.

- Grandin, Temple & Panek, Richard. (2013) *The autistic brain. Helping different kinds of minds succeed.* Houghton, Mifflin, Harcourt Publishing Company. New York.

- Jensen, Cory Jewell. (2016) *S/Os in the faith community* Discipleship Workshop, Oregon Camp Meeting, Gladstone. July 21, 2016.

- Lopez, Ana. (2016) *Pedophiles need help not hatred!* https://youtu.be/_SLInP3Jy9k. April 2016.

- McBride Wilson, Alex. (2016) *Beyond choice and reason. Non-offending paedephilia.* http://www.flintmag.com/portfolio/beyond-choice-non-offending-paedophilia/ April 18, 2016

- Palmer, Brian. (2010) *How do doctors treat pedophiles? With drugs, psychotherapy or scalpels.* http://www.slate.com/articles/news_and_politics/explainer/2010/03/how_do_doctors_treat_pedophiles.html. March 26, 2010.

- Quinn, Kenneth. (2015) *Mind of a Molester.* AuthorHouse, Bloomington, IN

- Seto, M. (2016) *The puzzle of male chronophilias.* Archives of Sexual Behavior. August 2016.

- Singal, Jesse. (2016) *Judges are starting to question overzealous sex-offender laws.* NYmag.com/daily/intelligence/2016/08/judges-are-questioning-overzealous-sex-offender-laws.html. August 29, 2016.

- StopSO (2016) Specialist Treatment Organisation for the Prevention of Sexual Offending. *StopSO.org.uk*

- Stanphill, Ira F. (1946) *Room at the Cross for You* http://lyricsplayground.com/alpha/songs/r/roomatt hecrossforyou.shtml

- Tabachnick, Joan & Klein, Alicia. (2011) *A reasoned approach: Reshaping S/O policy to prevent child sexual abuse.* Association for the Treatment of Sexual Abusers (ATSA) policy paper. Retrieved July 8, 2011 from http://www.atsa.com/pdfs/ppReasonedApproach.pd f.

- Tourjee, Diana. (2016) *Most Child Sex Abusers are Not Pedophiles.* Broadly. https://broadly.vice.com/en_us/article/most-child-sex-abusers-are-not-pedophiles-expert-says. April 4, 2016.

- Tucker, Mike. (2016)*Salvation Stories, Called Together.* Oregon Camp Meeting, Gladstone. July 22, July 23, 2016.

- Upadhye, Janet. (2016) *"I'm not a monster": A pedophile on attraction, love and a life of loneliness.* http://www.salon.com/2016/05/17/im_not_a_mon

ster_a_pedophile_on_attraction_love_and_a_life_of_loneliness/ May 17, 2016.

- VarmitCoyote, (2013) *Can you sympathize?* (Pedophiles ≠ Molesters) https://www.youtube.com/watch?v=PC0uuPD1a8g &feature=youtu.be. May 5, 2013.

- Yancey, Philip. (1998) CHURCH: why bother? p.42. Zondervan, Grand Rapids, MI.

Made in the USA
Middletown, DE
05 October 2021

49713799R00109